WE'RE JUST GOOD FRIENDS

THE GUILFORD SERIES
ON PERSONAL RELATIONSHIPS

Steve Duck, *Editor*
Department of Communication Studies, The University of Iowa

We're Just Good Friends

Women and Men in Nonromantic Relationships

KATHY WERKING

The Guilford Press
New York London

© 1997 The Guilford Press
A Division of Guilford Publications, Inc.
72 Spring Street, New York, NY 10012

Printed in the United States of America

This book is printed on acid-free paper.

Last digit is print number: 9   8   7   6   5   4   3   2   1

Library of Congress Cataloging-in-Publication Data

Werking, Kathy
    We're just good friends : women and men in nonromantic
relationships / Kathy Werking.
      p.   cm.—(The Guilford series on personal relationships)
    Includes bibliographical references and index.
    ISBN 1-57230-187-2
    1. Friendship.   2. Man–woman relationships.   I. Title.
II. Series.
BF575.F66W47   1997
306.73—dc21   97-2904
                                                CIP

Contents

WE'RE JUST GOOD FRIENDS

Introduction

Interviewer

Do you think that nonromantic friendship between a man and a woman is possible?

Male interviewee

Yes.

Interviewer

And why is that?

Male interviewee

'Cause they are people too. I don't see where sex has to do with whether they are your friend or not.

Interviewer

Do you have any close friends who are female?

Male interviewee

No.

The number of studies examining friendship has increased noticeably in the past decade. Such study could be characterized as trivial (O'Connor, 1992) since the research concerns itself with an emotional relationship whose status in the social world remains fluid and largely undefined. Regardless of whether it is nebulous, however, friendship performs important (as well as mundane) service in the everyday lives of women and men. For example, friends provide comfort to each

1

other, listen, fight, enhance each other's feelings of self-worth, play, ease loneliness, and alter each other's ways of thinking. In addition, developmental and social psychologists widely recognize friendship's contributions to the social development and sense of well-being of women and men (e.g., Davis & Todd, 1985).

Because of friendship's salience in daily life, its study contributes significantly to an understanding of the texture of the social world. A survey of the burgeoning literature on friendship, however, would lead one to believe that friendship is not only most common but also only possible between persons of the same sex, since the overwhelming majority of these studies have focused on same-sex friendships. By and large, friendship *between* the sexes has been overlooked by almost all researchers, regardless of their discipline.

The research focus on same-sex friendship studies reflects the prevalence of same-sex friendship in American culture. All the same, friendships between men and women do get established. Indeed, Wright (1989) took an average of the noncollege samples of four studies (Bell, 1981a; Block, 1980; Booth & Hess, 1974; Rubin, 1985) and found that 40% of the men and 30% of the women reported having close cross-sex friendships. Also using an adult sample, Sapadin (1988) found that 89% of her sample of professional men and women reported having had cross-sex friendships. In college the frequency of cross-sex friendship appears to be even higher, as all of the undergraduate and male graduate students and 73% of the female graduate students participating in Rose's (1985) study claimed at least one close cross-sex friendship outside of their romantic relationships. These numbers were even greater in Buhrke and Fuqua's (1987) study, in which their sample of college men and women reported an average of more than three "close" cross-sex friends.

These percentages may be viewed in two ways. First, it seems that men and women are developing friendships with one another as opportunities for interaction increase in the workplace, educational settings, and the community. The percentages cited in the studies above illustrate this point clearly. A second more critical reading is that barriers to the establishment of cross-sex friendship seem to persist simultaneously for there is a sizable percentage of the people in the studies mentioned above who did *not* have close cross-sex friendships.

Further, existing studies indicate that more barriers to cross-sex friendship are erected as persons age and marry. The number of reported cross-sex friendships reported by married people in middle and late adulthood is significantly lower than the number reported by single persons in adolescence and early adulthood (e.g., Booth & Hess, 1974; Adams, 1985). These barriers reflect cultural assumptions about the types of relationships that may be formed between heterosexual women and men. Specifically, in American culture, adult women and men are expected to form romantic bonds rather than platonic bonds with one another. In addition, when persons are married, becoming friends with an opposite-sex person is considered somewhat taboo (Lampe, 1985).

Given the strength of these cultural norms, many interesting questions for cross-sex friends arise: How do I know that the behaviors of an opposite sex person are "friendly" rather than "romantic" in nature? What do I say to my romantic partner when he or she is jealous of my cross-sex friendship? How do I preserve my cross-sex friendship when my cross-sex friend expresses a romantic interest in me? What will others think if I become friends with a married coworker?

Cross-sex friendship also poses interesting research questions: How do cultural assumptions about heterosexual relationships influence people's willingness to enter into cross-sex friendships? For those who do embark on cross-sex friendships, what are its characteristics? What difficulties threaten the viability of cross-sex friendships? Researchers know little about the answers to these questions because cross-sex friendships have only recently become the subject of focused investigation (e.g., Monsour, 1992; Werking, 1992).

This ignorance is unfortunate for several reasons. First, the new research is beginning to suggest that the dynamics of cross-sex friendship differ from those of same-sex friendship. These differences, as well as the similarities between the two types of friendship, need to be understood thoroughly if we want to understand friendship in general. Further, the existence of cross-sex friendship invites analysis of the cultural norms for conducting man–woman relationships since cross-sex friendship challenges the normative heterosexual romantic relationship. Finally, cross-sex friendship raises many important questions regarding the role of gender in the management of friendship as men and women interact with one another across boundaries that have normally existed between them. In sum, cross-sex friendship provides an arena in which to study the intersection of gender role expectations, relationship norms and goals, cultural assumptions, sexuality, and individual subjective experience.

Throughout the book, I use the term *gender* instead of *sex*. Historically, there has not been clarity nor consistency in the ways in which these terms have been used by researchers; therefore, I believe my terminology in this book should be explained. I use *gender* because the concept implies socially constructed modes of behavior rather than the biologically derived characteristics associated with *sex* (Wood, 1993). Further, I view gender as a relational construct rather than an individual construct. In other words, I conceptualize gender not as a static characteristic brought *to* relationships but as a fluid construct produced *through* interaction with others (Deaux & Major, 1987; West & Fenstermaker, 1995). Even though I use *gender* when writing about the behaviors of men and women in friendship, I will continue to use the term *cross-sex* friendship rather than *cross-gender* friendship because I mean simply that the friends are of different biological sexes.

The purposes of this book are fourfold. My first goal is to summarize what is known about cross-sex friendship, integrating studies conducted in sociology, psychology, and communication. This summary will include critical evaluation of the existing literature and suggestions for overcoming biases and limiting methodological practices.

A second goal is to present a description of the lived character of cross-sex friendship in order to enhance understanding of this type of friendship. My description ranges from the everyday activities of cross-sex friends to a focus on the various problematics challenging these friends. I am committed to offering descriptions close to the experiences of the participants in cross-sex friendship; therefore, the cross-sex friendship issues highlighted in this book are those that seemed most important to the women and men with whom I and other cross-sex friendship scholars have conducted research. These issues include dealing with sexual and romantic feelings in cross-sex friendship, handling jealous romantic partners, managing other persons' scrutiny of the friendship, and comparing the behavior of men and women in same-sex and cross-sex friendships.

Throughout the book, I draw heavily from surveys and in-depth interviews that I have conducted with cross-sex friends (the protocols along with descriptions of the studies are provided in the appendices). During the past 4 years, I have conducted in-depth interviews with 190 adults and surveyed 636 others about their close cross-sex friendships. Frequently, I present extended, unaltered quotations from those interviews and surveys to give the reader access to the friendship world of the participating men and women. Although the research that I have conducted provides much of the data upon which I base my descriptions of cross-sex friendship, these descriptions will be supported, questioned, and enriched by the results of cross-sex friendship studies conducted by other researchers.

A third goal of this book is to contribute to future cross-sex friendship studies by detailing a framework for conducting research in a manner not yet offered by existing research. In this regard, I made two decisions that have profoundly influenced my work on cross-sex friendship. First, I chose to view cross-sex friendship as a web of relationships, consisting of interconnections among the friends, third parties, the social structure, and the culture. Further, I chose to view these relationships as open-ended in nature. Because of these decisions, describing cross-sex friendship becomes a difficult and complex task.

The task is arduous in large part because our language does not afford a good range of terms for discussing this kind of relationship. In this regard, I have not transcended my culture nor the bulk of my education, both of which have equipped me with a vocabulary rich in individualistic terms and poor in terms describing relationship, complexity, and process. This poverty has been lamented for decades by a few relational researchers. In 1963, Haley claimed that we lack the needed terminology to talk about relationships. In backing up that claim, he pointed to the concepts that were prevalent in the psychological literature at the time. These concepts included *role, attitude, trait, cognition,* all of which he termed "inside skin" concepts. Haley's claims were echoed by Gottman (1982) who described researchers as being in the middle of a conceptual storm. Gottman asserted that the search for a language that adequately describes relationships has been frustrated by 2,300 years of research focused on the individual.

Recently, researchers have begun the search for ways to describe relationships between people as the relationships evolve over time. I am deeply grateful for the work of two of these scholars, Gregory Bateson and William Rawlins, because their writings not only provide me with "new ways of seeing" relationships but also provide me with the language tools to begin to describe what I see.

A second ramification of adopting the above perspective is that there is difficulty in presenting my descriptions of cross-sex friendship. I have chosen to highlight separately each aspect of the complex nature of cross-sex friendship and describe it in depth before moving on to another aspect. In many ways, this is a simple, linear way of describing a decidedly complex, nonlinear experience. This complexity will be evident for, at various moments in the book, I will defer discussion of related phenomena to a later section. This deferral may frustrate the reader at times, but I find it impossible to examine the parts without referring to the whole, or connected parts. The risk inherent in this strategy is that the sense of interdependency will be lost. Nevertheless, given the medium of presentation, this is the nature of the following descriptions.

The final goal of this book is to raise interest in the study of cross-sex friendship and in the forms and functions of cross-sex friendship in our everyday lives. In other words, I wish to "jump-start" the conversation about woman–man friendships since dialogue about this form of friendship is largely absent in the general population as well as in scholarly circles. To that end, I begin by articulating a framework for studying cross-sex friendship.

The chapters in this book articulate an organizational framework for theorizing about cross-sex friendship. This framework addresses several layers of analysis. These levels of analysis range from the individual level to the societal level. In addition to articulating various levels of analysis, the framework also explores the interconnections between these levels. The following section describes the framework in general terms. Subsequent chapters of this book provide specific examples of how the framework may be used as an organizing tool.

A CONCEPTUAL FRAMEWORK FOR INVESTIGATING CROSS-SEX FRIENDSHIP

Cross-sex friendship occupies a particular status in the social world. That is, it is a relationship within a whole system of relationships (Roberts, 1982). Since cross-sex friendship stands *in relation* to a system of recognized relationships in American society, it must be understood in the context of this system.

Systems of relationships are created via persons' mutual actions, or social practices (Taylor, 1977). For analytical purposes, social practices can be divided into two interrelated levels: relational practices and societal practices. *Relational practices* are the mutually negotiated and performed acts of partners engaged in a specific relationship that serve to create a matrix of intersubjective meanings unique to that relationship. *Societal practices* can be seen as metapatterns of relational practices (Bateson, 1978) since societal practices are the socially patterned relations among the patterned relations of partners in interaction with one another (Wilson, 1970). At this level, relationships are "ideals" and imply not only particular configurations of relations between persons and their encompassing social orders but also norms for behavior (Taylor, 1977).

Relational practices and societal practices are linked because, although there are ideal conceptions of relationships guiding humans as they relate to one another, there are also the real practices of relational partners that either sustain, reproduce, or contradict these ideals. An examination of the societal and relational practices of friendship will serve as an example of the linkage between the two levels.

The societal practice of friendship in the United States and in other Western cultures typically implies a particular relationship between persons, one that is equal and voluntary in nature. In addition, a set of idealized norms, such as reciprocity, trustworthiness, and loyalty, informs the practice of friendship. Also indicated in the conventional enactment of friendship is a normative relationship between friends and society. In other words, the ongoing accomplishment of friendship reflects a particular position for friendship vis-à-vis other relationships in the society, such as kin or business relationships (Paine, 1974). For example, kin are given priority over friends in American society, as evidenced by the popular saying, "Blood is thicker than water."

In the instance of friendship, relational practices involve the acts of "being a friend to a particular other." Friends create distinct ways of relating within their friendship. The societal context does not *determine* relational practices since friends bring to their interactions their own beliefs, interpretations, attitudes, and goals. In fact, societal practices are re-created continually as persons enact "friendship" with one another and are subject to alteration as a result of substantial changes in relational practices (Rawlins, 1989a). In other words, our ideal conceptions of friendship may be altered as persons forge different modes of enacting friendship.

Thus, each friendship interaction involves the interplay of both persons' subjective experiences and their meanings within the present relational context, which partly depends on past interactions in the current friendship and in the friends' other relationships. Further, friends and outsiders to the friendship interpret the meaning of these unique rituals, nicknames, and conversations to a significant degree in light of accepted cultural configurations of interpersonal relationships and their attendant norms.

As demonstrated above, societal practices inform the enactment of relational practices. Societal practices and relational practices are conceptually distinct levels of abstraction and analysis, yet they remain interrelated. Bateson (1991a) states:

> Insofar then as every event carries information about its context, we must grant that every event is relevant, i.e., carries information about every step of that infinite series which is the hierarchy of contexts. In this sense, every event becomes INFORMATIONALLY relevant to the whole universe (which is not the same as causally relevant). (pp. 143–144)

Hence, the search for understanding of the meaning of the relational practices of friends must also address and describe the societal practices associated with friendship. For example, the willingness of my friend to loan me money even though I cannot pay him back in the near future is rendered understandable to me when I consider two hallmarks of the ideal friend relationship: (1) the willingness to sacrifice for one's friends and (2) trust. In loaning me the money, my friend is acting *as a friend should* in this situation.

The search for understanding of the actions of friends is also a goal of friendship researchers. Following Bateson's lead, I contend that our understanding of these practices will be richer if we also consider the societal practices associated with friendship. Specifically, our interpretations and descriptions of the information provided to us by our research participants will be more robust if we anchor those interpretations to the societal and cultural context within which the relational practices take place.

The framework presented here divides social practices into the microlevel of relational practices and the macrolevel of societal practices. Even so, it avoids the classic micro–macro duality since the focus of investigation is directed toward the "middle ground" or what the Maines calls "meso" orders (Maines, 1982, 1989). That is, the framework focuses on the inherent dialectical relation between societal and relational practices. Specifically, I emphasize (1) the contradictions between expectations surrounding friendship as an ideal and (2) the daily realities of being friends, as well as the ongoing interpretive process of managing this dialectic (Rawlins, 1989a, 1992). Maines (1989) summarizes Rawlins's (1989a) conceptualization of this interpretive process in the following way:

> Friendship is a process as well as a form of creation and the creation and re-creation of a form. It is a pattern of participation that cannot be separated from other patterns of participation . . . it is a continuous interpretive process that is shaped in part by built-in incompatibilities . . . it is temporal . . . and it is reflexive. . . . In this perspective, ambiguity and uncertainty are lodged in movement and the multiple contexts of friendship formation and maintenance. Together ambiguity and uncertainty generate an ongoing interpretive problematic. (p. 192)

In sum, this framework consists of a multilayered analysis of the communicative experiences of cross-sex friends in present-day middle-class American society. In addition to addressing various levels of analysis, the framework weaves these levels together so that the focus of study becomes the interplay between levels. That is to say, research conducted within this framework seeks to illuminate the ways in which persons manage the occasionally divergent requirements of social, relational, and personal expectations. Viewed in this way, the management of cross-sex friendship becomes complex and dynamic in nature.

In Chapter 1, I examine one level of analysis as I explore the societal context in which cross-sex friendship is practiced. Chapter 1 articulates a structural analysis of the links between cross-sex friendships and other important personal relationships, namely, romantic heterosexual relationships and same-sex friendships. In this chapter, I discuss how heterosexism infuses the everyday enactment of cross-sex friendships.

Subsequent chapters constitute a second avenue of analysis as they examine persons' descriptions of the relational practices constituting cross-sex friendship. These practices reflect the strategic choices of cross-sex friends as they negotiate their friendships amidst varying configurations of social and personal circumstances. Accordingly, the chapters focus on issues relevant to the development, sustenance, and demise of cross-sex friendships. Chapters 2, 3, and 4 address the private side of cross-sex friendship, focusing on specific cross-sex friendship issues that may arise during the lifetime of a friendship.

Chapter 2 describes the conversational content and the activities of cross-sex friends, as well as the influence of gender on the character of cross-sex friendship. Chapter 3 focuses on the development and dissolution of cross-sex friendship, articulating the internal and external patterns that impede or facilitate this process.

Chapter 4 investigates how cross-sex friends manage issues of romance and sexuality in their friendships. The terms *sex* and *romance* were usually used interchangeably by the persons who participated in my studies. In their view, acting on sexual attraction transformed a friendship between a man and a woman into a romantic relationship. Further, a lack of sexual attraction made a romantic relationship improbable. Thus, I have linked the two issues as well. The emphasis of this chapter is on the management of these issues in friendships between heterosexual men and women. This chapter is, in large part, a reflection of the heterosexism found in American culture and in the research literature. In Chapter 1, I detail the ways in which heterosexism is evident in our culture. Then, in Chapter 4, I discuss how heterosexism (1) informs my own study as well as the work of others and (2) may be overcome in our future work.

Chapter 5 examines the public aspect of cross-sex friendship by describing how both cross-sex friends manage their obligations to multiple relationships and rhetorically create a public image of their friendship that is viewed as authentic and legitimate by third parties. Throughout these chapters, I will juxtapose the descriptions of actual cross-sex friendships with the more generalized societal images of cross-sex friendship presented in Chapter 1. Lastly, the Conclusion reviews the major points of the book, critically examines the cross-sex friendship literature, and poses questions for future research.

Before each chapter, I include segments of conversations between cross-sex friends. At the time that this discourse occurred, these men and women had been close friends for an average of 3½ years, and their ages ranged from 20 to 37 years. While selecting this sample, I strove to represent several variations of cross-sex friendship composition. For example, I had two friendship dyads that consisted of a homosexual man and a heterosexual woman; one friendship was a cross-racial as well as a cross-sex friendship; and, while the majority of the friendship dyads consisted of persons who were single, in several dyads one of the friends was married.

The 15-minute conversations were tape-recorded following interviews with both friends. Prior to leaving the room, the interviewer made some suggestions about topics that the friends might wish to discuss but stressed that their conversations did not need to be limited to these topics. These conversations reflect the issues highlighted in this book and allow the reader to see how persons actually involved in close cross-sex friendships talk about them.

1

The Societal Context of Cross-Sex Friendship

Comparisons with Paradigmatic Social Relationships

ANNE AND CARL

Anne and Carl, both 23 years old, are white, single, college students. Carl revealed to Anne 6 years into their friendship that he is gay. Anne and Carl have been close friends for 10 years.

Anne

> Well, the weird thing was, when I was in high school, my parents always thought it was weird that you were such good friends with me. . . . They always thought it was strange that you were such good friends with me. And I'm like, "I guess this just proves that you can be friends with a guy and not be romantically involved."
>
> Because my dad was just raised as how . . . if you . . . if you have a relationship with a woman, it's something romantic. Either that, or it's a work relationship.

Carl

> Yeah. 'Cause my grandparents and stuff would always say things like . . .

Anne

> 'Cause the females my dad is involved with . . . if he's good friends with them, it's always in the context of her and her

husband, my mom and my dad. And he's just, like, joking or flirting or something like that with her. But it's nothing like he would . . . he has no real female relationship where he'd call her up and they'd go out to a movie and it would be no big deal. I mean, that is not even a possibility for my dad.

Carl

Yeah. My grandparents would always . . . they'd say something like, call you my girlfriend and stuff. Or even people at school! . . .

Anne

Everybody at school!

Carl

. . . thought that we were dating. *(Laughs)*

Anne

Granted we did spend all of our time together, and we did share a locker. But . . . *(Laughs)*

Carl

Everybody thought we were . . .

Anne

Looking back, I can see how they would think that. I mean, 'cause I found myself saying, "Well, they spend all their time together, they must be dating." And then I think, "Well, I guess that's not true because look at me and Carl."

Carl

People just naturally assume that you're having like a . . . like sex too, if you're friends.

Anne

I think it's better now than when our parents grew up.

Carl

Mm hmm.

Anne

I mean, in our generation, I think we . . . I can see almost a majority of the people not really having a problem with cross-sex friendships. I mean, not really seeing anything wrong with it or totally accepting it.

Carl

Even if I see . . . even if I see older people, like an older man or a woman together, I just assume that they're married. It never even enters my mind that they might just be friends.

Anne

Really?

Carl

Yeah. I don't think that ever enters my mind. Like when you wait on people, if they're together. I mean like if they're younger kids or so. But if they're older people, I just assume they're married.

Anne

Yeah. Yeah.

Carl

Like I had a couple the other night. They turned out to be cousins, but they just sat down, and I was like, "This looks like a nice, married couple." And then I was talking to them, and they were like, "Oh, we're cousins. We're just friends." And I was like, "Oh, *Oh.*" It just never . . . that's the first thing I think. I guess it enters my mind. But that's the first thing I think when I see, like, an older couple.

Anne

Yeah, but when I see people our age together, I always wonder, "Well, they could be brother and sister, they could be friends, they could be dating." I mean, I always wonder. 'Cause you can't . . . it's not . . . like I think earlier in the century if you saw two people our age together, you'd just automatically think that they were dating or whatever. Now, I always wonder, I always question.

Carl

Yeah. I, like, wonder when you and I would go into the cafeteria and, like, sit down and stuff and people were, like . . . what they thought about us. I guess they probably did think that we were boyfriend and girlfriend. 'Cause I was always, like, throwing bread in your hair! *(Laughs)* I guess people probably do, like, figure that we're dating when we go out.

The conversation between Anne and Carl highlights many of the quandaries associated with cross-sex friendship in middle-class American society. Historically, intimate relationships between men and women in American society have been limited to romantic or kin relationships. In recent years, however, friendship has become an alternative relational option between men and women. Even so, this option has been approached with trepidation as people begin to shed long-held beliefs about man–woman relationships. Such apprehension is expressed in the talk of Anne and Carl as they describe repeatedly how others view their relationship as "weird" or as a dating relationship.

Even though Anne and Carl are involved in an intimate friendship, they also have difficulty making sense of others' relationships. They find themselves questioning the nature of the man–woman relationships that they see at work and school. Many people still believe that man–woman friendships are simply incipient romantic relationships. Others question whether men and women have enough in common to be friends.

This chapter situates cross-sex friendship in this social world by comparing it to other forms of intimate relationships. These comparisons seek to answer the following questions: How does a cross-sex friendship compare with a heterosexual romantic relationship? What influence does the heterosexual romantic ideology exert on possibilities for woman–man friendship? How does cross-sex friendship compare with same-sex friendship, the most common form of friendship? Comparing cross-sex friendship with other relational forms is useful, for, as Weston (1991) notes, "In any relational definition, the juxtaposition of two terms gives meaning to both. Just as light would not be meaningful without some notion of darkness" (p. 28). Thus, this chapter seeks to illuminate experiences that are unique to cross-sex friendship and those that are common to other types of relationships so that we may begin to learn what it means to be friends with members of the opposite sex.

A sustained consideration of the character, problems, activities, and rewards of cross-sex friendship must start with an analysis of its niche in the social system or, as described in the Introduction to this book, at the level of societal practices. I will first detail the character of friendship in modern-day middle-class American society and demonstrate how friendship between persons of the same sex constitutes the paradigmatic friend relationship. Then I will turn our attention to the paradigmatic romantic heterosexual relationship in contemporary middle-class American society. I will discuss its norms, goals, and status vis-à-vis other social relationships in order to demonstrate how cross-sex friendship compares with this normative relationship.

THE NATURE OF FRIENDSHIP

Friendship is typically thought of as a voluntary relationship. Since there are few formal rules or rituals sanctioning friendship in this culture, people enter and exit friendships as they choose (Simmel, 1971). Further, since "friendship" is often fused with other social roles, marital partners, siblings, or coworkers often choose to regard one another as "friends." Acknowledging that friendship is culturally recognized as transcending formal institutional requirements and statuses, Paine (1974) referred to friendship as a "kind of institutionalized non-institution" (p. 128). In other words, friendship courses through our lives, yet its precise nature is difficult to define.

In addition to its voluntary aspect, friendship involves persons paired in the same social role (friend–friend) (Paine, 1974). This quality contrasts with other relationships, such as the marital relationship, in which partners occupy complementary roles (wife–husband). Because of friendship's inherent symmetry, friends come together as *equals* in order to establish a relationship in which intimacy, trust, honesty, respect, and affection may thrive (Simmel, 1971). Ideally, friendship offers a nonhierarchical relationship in which a person can present a self reasonably "free of contrivance and ulterior motives"

(Suttles, 1970, p. 110). While developing and sustaining a friendship, persons must assume that the other is presenting his or her "true" self if the friendship is to flourish.

Reflecting its voluntary and rather fluid status in the social world, friendship is a private relationship created via the friends' ongoing negotiation of the friendship's "rules of relevancy," or rules of behavior (Paine, 1974). Friendships are thus "self-managed" (Wiseman, 1986, p. 192) since specific friendship practices are not mandated by formal societal rules in American culture. Friends are free to create their own private and personal culture. But this freedom is also dangerous, for the persistence of the relationship utterly depends on the friends' actions, values, and motives. Thus, friendship is arguably the most fragile social bond. Wiseman (1986) states that if friendship

> loses the qualities which make for the extraordinary closeness combined with the voluntariness it encourages, it chances loss of all. There is no standard role or task around which the relationship can re-form and no societal mechanism is activated to ensure or even encourage reconciliation. (p. 192)

Although the precise behavioral parameters of friendship are not institutionalized in American society to the degree that romantic, professional, political, or kin relationships are, we can refer to informal rules of conduct and cultural images guiding the practices of friendship. For example, a study by Argyle and Henderson (1985) found 21 highly endorsed rules associated with same-sex friendship. These rules pertained to keeping confidences, respecting the other's privacy, and assisting the other in times of need.

Further, there is a set of cultural expectations associated with friendship (Rawlins, 1989a) as persons are "socialized into normative expectations regarding certain ideal conceptions and practices of friendship" (Rawlins, 1989a, p. 167). Current images of friendship are evident in studies in which adults have been questioned about their conceptions of the relationship. These studies have found that across adulthood, friends are described as loyal and warm (Parlee, 1979), trustworthy and easy to talk to (Crawford, 1977), and dependable (e.g.,

Candy, Troll, & Levy, 1981; Tesch & Martin, 1983). Moreover, these idealized friendship qualities seem to be important to both men and women (Rose, 1985; Tesch & Martin, 1983).

The culturally idealized images of friendship and the informal friendship rules offer persons ways of practicing friendship, for those images and rules frame the everyday enactment of friendship. The interactions of friends are understood to a significant degree in light of what it means to "be a friend" in a particular society. Idealized images and informal rules may also guide the perceptions of observers, for, when questioned about their friendship, friends may point to these cultural images of friendship or to the rules of friendship behavior to validate their friendship (Suttles, 1970).

SAME-SEX FRIENDSHIP AS THE PARADIGMATIC FRIEND RELATIONSHIP

It is possible, however, that these cultural images of friendship are idealized images of *same-sex friendship* rather than images of cross-sex friendship because of the prevalence of same-sex friendship in this culture. For example, when idealized conceptions of friendship have been gathered and studied, researchers have either directed participants to describe the ideal same-sex friend or have simply asked the participants to define a "friend." This option might only elicit descriptions of same-sex friendship as well, for, as Hess (1972) states, "The fusion of friendship with the sex role is so nearly complete through most of the life course that 'friend' in popular usage . . . generally refers to another of the same sex" (p. 364).

Thus, the paradigmatic friend relationship is the friendship between members of the same sex. Since cross-sex friendship does not fit neatly into middle-class American society's conception of friendship, the following questions demand consideration: What cultural images and rules of friendship do cross-sex friends point to when validating their relationship? Is cross-sex friendship a part of our cultural conversation? If so, how do we talk about it? How do these images influence the everyday practices of cross-sex friends? These questions pose important issues, because without a "vision" of cross-sex friendship the possibility of this type of friendship might not be apparent to members of this culture and the viability of established woman–man friendships might be undermined.

Historically, same-sex friendships have been encouraged for both men and women, but for different reasons. Because of the societal valuation of men over women, men have been encouraged to form friendships with other men. Men offered each other economic, political, legal, educational, and occupational resources that women could not offer (Rose, 1985). Women could not develop friendships with men because of the inherent egalitarian nature of friendship. Since it was believed that women had nothing of value to offer men, friendship between the sexes was not a possibility. In addition, opportunities for the formation of friendships between men and women were rare since women were relegated to the private sphere of the home rather than the public sphere of the workplace. Accordingly, women turned to other women for friendship, where they received emotional support, validation of self-worth, and companionship (Faderman, 1989; de Beauvoir, 1952).

Although boundaries between the sexes are not as rigid today, both women and men continue to seek friendships primarily with members of their own sex. Cross-sex friendship in childhood and preadolescence is rare (Gottman, 1986). Studies indicate that the preference for friendships with same-sex others increases dramatically from 3 years of age to 7 or 8 years of age (Gottman, 1986; Maccoby, 1988). Maccoby (1988) reports that 4-year-olds play 3 times as much with same- as with cross-sex children but that 6-year-olds play 11 times as much with same- as compared with cross-sex peers. Taken together, the existing studies demonstrate clearly that sex is a prime organizer of friend relationships throughout childhood (Cohen, D'Heurle, & Widmark-Peterson, 1980; Gottman, 1986; Smith & Inder, 1990).

During middle childhood, cross-sex relationships yield to same-sex relationships (Gottman & Mettetal, 1986). Cross-sex interactions are often antagonistic in nature, marked by teasing, usually in the form of insults about physical attributes or threats about liking someone of the opposite sex (Gottman & Mettetal, 1986). Children also view the opposite sex as incompatible because of a lack of shared characteristics (e.g., interest in similar activities, physical abilities) (Smith & Inder, 1990). Friendship with the opposite sex then is unlikely through preadolescence because of the negative affect typifying cross-sex relationships.

The negative evaluation of the opposite sex is softened during adolescence as indicated by the rise in cross-sex friendship occurrence (Kon & Losenkov, 1978; Sharabany, Gershoni, & Hoffman, 1981). The number of cross-sex friendships, however, does not compete with the number of same-sex friendships. For example, Kon and Losenkov (1978) found two to four times more same-sex friendships than cross-sex friendships. Further, the intimacy of this type of friendship does not approach the intimacy of same-sex friendship (Sharabany et al., 1981). These findings led Sharabany et al. (1981) to conclude:

> The transition from preadolescence to adolescence is marked by an increase in all aspects of intimate friendship with the opposite sex, thus suggesting that whereas same-sex intimacy is already in process, opposite-sex relations are in their initial phase. (p. 604)

Most of the studies of cross-sex friendship in childhood and adolescence have taken place in schools, a context that promotes segregation of the sexes and exerts strong pressure by the peer group (Thorne, 1986). The context of study, therefore, might be a factor in the extremely low number of cross-sex friendships reported by children in middle childhood and preadolescence. Researchers who have broadened their focus to include neighborhood and out-of-school activities have found that cross-sex friendships are more prevalent, though still not commonplace, outside of school (Maccoby, 1988; Smith & Inder, 1990; Thorne, 1986). Interestingly, cross-sex friendships that thrive outside of the school environment go "undercover" during the school day because of the negative sanctions imposed by the peer group (Gottman, 1986; Thorne, 1986).

In sum, it appears that girls and boys are not inclined to forge friendships with one another until they reach adolescence.

By that time, friendships within the same-sex group have become the paradigmatic friendship for members and may in turn be used as a standard when evaluating cross-sex interactions (Rose, 1985). The desirability and availability of same-sex friendship does not dissipate in adulthood but becomes more pronounced throughout the life span as evidenced by the percentages of adults reporting cross-sex friendships, cited in the Introduction to this book (see Wright, 1989). Studies indicate that as persons marry and age the number of reported cross-sex friendships decreases (Booth & Hess, 1974; Rose, 1985; Rubin, 1985), so that in late adulthood man–woman friendships are rarely established (Adams, 1985; Chown, 1981). In Chapter 3, I will discuss the explanations offered by researchers for this decline.

From childhood through later adulthood, persons engage in same-sex friendships far more frequently than cross-sex friendships. Consequently, men and women "know" how to be friends with a same-sex person because of their multiple and varied experiences with the same-sex type of friendship. The comfort that such knowledge produces may lead to a self-perpetuating cycle of avoidance of cross-sex friendship; a person may not venture into friendship with the opposite sex because of a lack of experience with cross-sex friendship.

Mirroring everyday life, researchers have implicitly adopted same-sex friendship as the paradigmatic friend relationship. They have conducted studies that compare cross-sex friendship with same-sex friendship, seeking to find the ways in which cross-sex friendship deviates from the model of same-sex friendship. In the following section, I will review studies that have compared the affective qualities of cross-sex friendship in general with same-sex friendship. Even so, limited and narrow information exists about the nature of cross-sex friendship and how friendship that reaches across sexual boundaries compares to within-sex friendship. Nevertheless, what is known points to consistent differences in the affective nature of cross-sex and same-sex friendship and suggests the existence of a unique cultural model of cross-sex friendship.

CROSS-SEX FRIENDSHIP AND SAME-SEX FRIENDSHIP COMPARED

Persons's conceptions specifically of cross-sex friendship have been elicited by only one study (Werking, 1992). This study suggests that persons who have experienced a close friendship with a cross-sex person have idealized images of cross-sex friendship that are similar to same-sex friendship. The participants mentioned honesty, openness, dependability, reciprocity, and acceptance as qualities that they expect to find in a same-sex friendship. When asked to describe their expectations of cross-sex friendship, the following excerpts were typical responses:

"I just expect them to be my friend and nothing more, nothing less really. I wouldn't expect anything more out of them either than I would out of any of my girlfriends. Just to be there when I want to talk to them, and I'll be there for them." *(Woman)*

"I don't really think about a female or male aspect, you know, a friend is a friend." *(Man)*

"Basically the same as a female. Just somebody you can count on and they won't hurt you, and you know that they'll be there when you need them." *(Woman)*

"Just like with any good friend, we can talk about anything, . . . hanging around, doing fun stuff, they're just the same." *(Man)*

"I think that the characteristics of a cross-sex friend as opposed to my other male friends, you know, would be, would be the same. Sex has nothing to do with it." *(Man)*

These descriptions suggest that the sexual composition of the friendship dyad exerts little influence on the participants' conceptions of the friendship. As the following review reveals, however, differences due to the sexual makeup of the friendship dyad do emerge when persons are asked to compare their *actual* experiences with same-sex and cross-sex friends.

Researchers in the 1980s turned their attention to comparing the affective qualities of cross-sex friendship with the affective qualities of same-sex friendship. These qualities have been measured by surveying participants about their cross-sex and same-sex friendships. The measured qualities include goodness and enjoyableness (Bukowski, Nappi, & Hoza, 1988), intimacy (Aukett, Ritchie, & Mill, 1988; Davis & Todd, 1985; Monsour, 1992; Rose, 1985; Sapadin, 1988), stability and supportiveness (Davis & Todd, 1985), loyalty (Rose, 1985), satisfaction (Argyle & Furnham, 1983), and self-disclosure (Hacker, 1981). These findings provide evidence that cross-sex friendships and same-sex friendships are not cut from the same cloth since respondents in all of these investigations reported significant differences between their same-sex and cross-sex friendships.

Taken together, the results of these studies show cross-sex friendships to be less intimate, less stable (Davis & Todd, 1985), less supportive (Rose, 1985), and less satisfying (Argyle & Furnham, 1983) than same-sex friendships. Levels of self-disclosure are also reduced in cross-sex friendships (Bell, 1981b; Hacker, 1981). In one study, participants revealed that they would disclose less to a cross-sex friend because of greater feelings of closeness with their same-sex friends and because of the jealousy of their romantic partners (Bell, 1981b).

Same-sex friends are perceived as more likely than cross-sex friends to interact with one another (Rands & Levinger, 1979) and to share similar interests. For example, Argyle and Furnham (1983) reported that same-sex friends scored higher than cross-sex friends on shared interests. This factor included items tapping shared activities, discussion of personal problems, shared friends, and working together. Conflict was also higher for cross-sex friends in this study. Increased conflict seemed to reflect reduced freedom in discussing personal problems with cross-sex friends and greater difficulty in understanding one another. These findings were supported in a later study by Rose (1985) who found that same-sex friends experienced more common interests, affection, acceptance, and communication than cross-sex friends did while developing and maintaining their friendships. Cross-sex friends, on the other hand, reported that greater time and sexual attraction was involved in their developing friendships. Rose (1985) sums up her findings regarding the differences between same-sex and cross-sex friendship:

> Cross-sex friendship formation and maintenance differs significantly from same-sex friendship in terms of the partners' high rate of statements concerning their unwillingness, lack of interest, or difficulty in forming and maintaining cross-sex friendship. (p. 72)

Based on these studies, cross-sex and same-sex friendship appear to be distinctive in several respects. However, similarities between the two types of friendship have been identified; therefore, these differences should not be overdrawn. It is also possible that in searching for differences, similarities have been ignored (Duck & Wright, 1993; Wright, 1988). For example, Davis and Todd (1985) found no differences between cross-sex and same-sex friendship in levels of trust, respect, acceptance, spontaneity, and enjoyment; yet these findings were virtually ignored in their discussion. Cross-sex and same-sex friends were nearly identical in the meanings that they assigned to intimacy in their friendships (Monsour, 1992). Nevertheless, differences between the actual experience of cross-sex and same-sex friendship are consistent across several studies even though persons may hold similar ideal images of the two friendship types.

In sum, we have seen that same-sex friendship is the most common form of friendship across the life course. In addition, research suggests that cross-sex friendship and same-sex friendship are not identical types of friendship since differences in affective characteristics have been revealed consistently across studies. These differences imply that the prevalence of same-sex friendship, coupled with the dominance of the romantic ideology in American middle-class culture, produces a different form of bond between male and female friends. Consequently, same-sex friendship experiences cannot entirely inform or guide cross-sex friendship experiences. I now compare cross-sex friendship with the heterosexual romantic relationship in order to illustrate how cross-sex friendship stands apart from this paradigmatic woman–man relationship and how the nature of cross-sex friendship is molded by the pervasiveness of the ideology of heterosexual romantic love.

THE ROMANTIC RELATIONSHIP AS A PARADIGMATIC MAN–WOMAN RELATIONSHIP

Romantic relationships are celebrated as an ideal woman–man relationship in our society. The myths of our culture secure a special status for romantic heterosexual relationships (Arliss, 1993) since these myths idealize romantic love and promote the notion that the emotional well-being of men and women is dependent upon their involvement in a "successful" romantic relationship (DiIorio, 1989). In essence, romanticism has become the reigning ideology for personal relationships between men and women (Brain, 1976) and is widely recognized as the primary basis for marriage. Further, women and men are encouraged to establish romantic relationships with one another and are provided models for establishing and sustaining these relationships by the media, family, friends, and the legal and educational system.

As a reigning relational ideology, romantic love is a social institution in this society (Brain, 1976; Van de Vate, 1981). Consequently, the behaviors associated with the development and maintenance of romantic relationships are specified and regulated to varying degrees of consciousness by dating and courtship scripts, rules, and rituals. These scripts, rules, and rituals provide guidelines for the production and interpretation of behavior in heterosexual romantic relationships. Part of the socialization process, therefore, includes learning and regulating the routines or scripts provided by the institution of heterosexual romantic love for reproducing itself. In fact, one of the functions of a social institution is to shape individuals' sense of "what is fitting, training them to find some actions and situations easeful and natural, others strained and uncomfortable" (Van de Vate, 1981, p. 71).

Dating is a primary activity of the institution of romantic love since dating is a way of getting to know a member of the opposite sex in the hopes of finding a suitable partner with whom to "fall in love." Falling in love is the primary reason for a couple's moving from the rather aimless activity of dating to the more serious relationship of courtship (Laws & Schwartz, 1981). The traditional model of dating was highly scripted. For example, males were expected to initiate the date and pay for expenses incurred on the date; females regulated the physical relationship; dates took place in prescribed locations; and the transition from a dating relationship to courtship was marked by widely recognized gestures and symbols (Cates & Lloyd, 1992).

Since marriage is its culturally endorsed goal, courtship has a series of socially recognized stages toward achieving that goal: going steady; in some cases, engagement and/or cohabitation; and, finally, marriage. Depending on the stage of courtship, certain behaviors are mandated between the partners. As the courtship approaches marriage, couples begin to take on more and more of the characteristics of married couples, with such patterns as the division of labor and the establishment of sexual activity (Laws & Schwartz, 1981).

Although the norms and rules directing persons along the path to marriage are less clear today than in the past (Cates & Lloyd, 1992), recent research indicates that adult men and women tend to hold traditional values concerning who should pay for dates, initiate sex, and propose marriage (Buhrke & Fuqua, 1987; Grauerholz & Serpe, 1985; McKinney, 1987). Such conservatism in courtship is also reflected in the resurgence of traditional dances, proms, and weddings in recent years (Gates & Lloyd, 1992). Finally, although the label of courtship seems outdated today, romantic love continues to be the core reason for the transition from a casual dating relationship to a "serious relationship" to marriage (Simpson, Campbell, & Berscheid, 1986).

With romantic love as their core and marriage as their goal, what is the nature of romantic heterosexual relationships? Researchers interested in delineating a paradigm case of romantic love relationships have identified the following characteristics: asymmetrical eligibilities, enjoyment, advocating/championing, giving the utmost, acceptance, respect, spontaneity, understanding, intimacy, fascination, and exclusiveness (see Table 1.1) (Davis & Todd, 1982; Roberts, 1982).

While these attributes are useful for understanding the nature of romantic relationships, the implications for relational partners involved in a relationship exhibiting such qualities are easily overlooked by merely listing the qualities. For example, exclusivity breeds possessiveness, and so the latter too is a quality of the romantic relationship (Horton, 1973). Closely linked with exclusivity and possessiveness is jealousy about time that one spends away from a romantic partner and vice versa or jealousy about attention that a romantic partner gives to persons who might be construed as rivals (see Aune & Comstock, 1991; Bringle & Boebinger, 1990). Second, asymmetrical eligibilities imply an "unequal playing field," or an imbalance of power within the relationship. Thus, romantic relationships are often the scene of power struggles as persons grapple with issues of dependency, control, and the management of relational resources (e.g., Argyle & Furnham, 1983). Third, unreciprocated sacrifice leads to loss of identity as well as to disappointment and pain.

Further, the paradigm case of romantic relationships overlooks other relational dynamics emanating from American culture's expecta-

TABLE 1.1. Paradigmatic Case Formulations of Romantic Love and Friendship

Davis & Todd (1982)	Roberts (1982)
Paradigm case—Romantic love	
Asymmetrical eligibilities	Asymmetrical eligibilities
Enjoyment	Intimacy
Advocating/championing	Respect
Give the utmost	Advocating/championing
Acceptance	Willingness to give utmost
Respect	Fascination
Spontaneity	Exclusivity
Understanding	
Fascination	
Exclusiveness	
Intimacy	
Paradigm case—Friendship	
Equal eligibilities	Symmetrical eligibilities
Enjoy	Intimacy
Trust	Respect
Mutual assistance	Trust
Respect	Liking
Spontaneity	
Understanding	
Intimacy	

tions of romantic relationships. Love and sexuality are fused together in the ideology of romance (Hendrick & Hendrick, 1992); therefore, issues of the nature and extent of sexuality become a part of romantic relationships. These issues are often not easily managed and may render the relationship vulnerable to dissolution. Finally, since romantic relationships are elevated to a primary position in the lives of men and women, members of romantic relationships are expected to forsake other relationships, such as friends, in order to spend time with their romantic partner (DiIorio, 1989; Rose, 1984; Rose & Serafica, 1986). Thus, involvement in a romantic relationship reduces persons' social networks—which, in turn, heightens the participants' emotional investment in the romantic relationship.

The potential for the above issues to become a part of a romantic relationship contributes to the volatility of romantic relationships. Davis and Todd (1985) clearly sum up the unstable character of romantic relationships when they state that "love relationships provide an excellent breeding ground for ambivalence and conflict" (p.26). Participants in romantic relationships experience great highs as well as great lows, in part because couples, particularly unmarried couples, are unable to predict the future outcome of the relationship with much certainty and because expectations about the relationship are lofty. The unpredictability of dating relationships was evidenced in a recent longitudinal study in which 42% of the romantic relationships that the participants had designated as their closest relationship (closer than friends or family) at the start of the research project dissolved during the 9-month period of the study (Berscheid, Snyder, & Omoto, 1989).

To summarize, we have seen that the romantic relationship is a paradigmatic relationship in this society and assumes prominence as the ideal woman–man relationship. Accordingly, the behaviors associated with developing and maintaining such a relationship are specified and regulated to varying degrees of consciousness by dating and courtship scripts and norms. We have also seen that romantic relationships, because of their unique status in this society and their associated expectations, are double-edged swords, simultaneously problematic and rewarding.

CROSS-SEX FRIENDSHIP AND ROMANTIC LOVE COMPARED

There are several similarities between the ideal/typical cross-sex friendship and the romantic heterosexual relationship. Both types of relationship are voluntary in nature, and friends and lovers are chosen because of desirable personal attributes. Further, feelings of affection and love are a part of both relationships. The extent and nature of these feelings in a friendship and romantic relationship are negotiated by the relational partners and may differ only in degree (Rawlins, 1982). Finally, cross-sex friendship and the romantic relationship require a substantial level of emotional energy if either type of relationship is to thrive (Rawlins, 1993).

Although cross-sex friendship is similar to the romantic heterosexual relationship in many respects, differences between the two types of relationship are apparent. First, cross-sex friendship is basically an attraction of the spirit, therefore, a strong sexual dimension is usually not present or is not allowed to be a part of the relationship (Rawlins, 1982). Sexuality may become a part of a cross-sex friend relationship, but its occurrence often signals the end of "friendship" and the beginning of a "love relationship" since romance and sexuality are so closely aligned in romantic ideology. Sexuality may also introduce feelings of possessiveness and jealousy. These types of feelings are downplayed in friendship; thus, their presence may destabilize a cross-sex friendship. Consequently, it is not surprising to find that men and women tend to keep their cross-sex friendships and sexual relationships separate, although sexual feelings and tensions remain present in their friendships (Sapadin, 1988; Werking, 1992, 1994a, 1994c).

Second, the goal of cross-sex friendship is not marriage. Instead, cross-sex friendship is an end unto itself rather than a means of achieving a greater goal (Badhwar, 1987). This distinction in relational goals may be the most profound difference between cross-sex friendship and the romantic relationship since men and women have been taught to expect that their intimate relationships with one another will lead to a particular end—marriage. In this regard, cross-sex friendship stands in direct opposition to the romantic ideology and its attendant kinship system. This resistance to the dominant ideology gives rise to much of the debate about whether or not women and men can, or should, be true friends.

Third, because of the fundamental nature of friendship discussed previously, cross-sex friendship is a relationship among equals. That is, men and women have equivalent behavioral opportunities, and the same behavior is considered appropriate for both the woman and the man (Roberts, 1982). As noted in my discussion of romantic heterosexual relationships, men and women do not hold the same status in these relationships. Accordingly, men and women are granted different behavioral opportunities and meanings. The equivalency inherent in cross-sex friendship resists patriarchical relationships between men and women and, therefore, contributes to the "subversive" nature of cross-sex friendship.

Finally, cross-sex friendship is not an exclusive relationship as is the romantic relationship. Cross-sex friends expect their partners to engage in other friendships, romantic relationships, and relationships with coworkers. Often, as indicated by my interviewees, cross-sex friends must negotiate how much time they can devote to the friendship given other demands in their lives. Although this freedom may threaten the existence of the cross-sex friendship, friends also recognize that their relationship is often enriched by participation in other relationships.

The above differences are reflected in the empirical research that compares friendship with the heterosexual romantic relationship (reviewed below). In the past decade, studies have compared friendship in general with the romantic relationship. The majority of the studies that compare friendship and the romantic heterosexual relationships utilize only same-sex friends in their samples or simply direct the participants to describe a "friend." A few studies have compared cross-sex friendships specifically with romantic relationships and have found significant differences in the nature of the two relational types (e.g., Argyle & Furnham, 1983; Davis & Todd, 1982, 1985; Rands & Levinger, 1979). Given my focus on cross-sex friendship, I will limit this review to those studies that have focused on cross-sex friendship and the romantic relationship.

The distinctions between cross-sex friendships and romantic heterosexual relationships are most clearly reflected in the work on relational paradigms by Davis and Todd (1982, 1985) and Roberts (1982) (see Table 1.1). These researchers strove to develop ideal/typical cases of each relational type and, therefore, delineated broad relational characteristics. Roberts's (1982) paradigm case is specific to cross-sex friendship, whereas Davis and Todd's (1982, 1985) work addresses friendship in general. I include Davis and Todd's (1982, 1985) formulation because their validation study addressed both same- and cross-sex friendship.

As noted in Table 1.1, Roberts (1982) and Davis and Todd (1982, 1985) listed symmetrical obligations as a basic feature of friendship. This feature means that, unlike the romantic relationship, men and women have the same opportunities and responsibilities in friendship. In other words, the "bargain" struck in friendship is other-oriented as well as self-oriented, for, as Paine (1974) states, "Each is concerned with their friend's side of the bargain as well as their own" (p. 512). This bargain is reflected in the mutual and reciprocal nature of exchanges found in friendship. Thus, the negotiation of these exchanges differs in kind from the negotiations of romantic partners described previously.

In addition to the basic dimension of relational eligibilities, the formulation of paradigm cases of relationships provides glimpses into other differences between friendship and the romantic heterosexual relationship. For example, the dimensions of "trust" and "mutual assistance" appear in the list for friendship but are absent in the romantic love relationship paradigm. Conversely, "exclusivity," "fascination," "advocating/championing," and "willingness to give utmost" appear as components of the love relationship, but not components of friendship.

Davis and Todd (1985) tested the validity of their paradigm case formulations with college students and were surprised by some of the results. First, the researchers had expected that spouses and lovers would be more likely than best friends to act as champions or advocates of their partner's interests. However, the data suggested that the reverse is true. Second, contradicting expectations, Davis and Todd (1985) found that their sample saw best friendships (both same-sex and cross-sex) as more stable than romantic relationships. Interestingly, this result also held for close same-sex friends, but not for close cross-sex friends. Davis and Todd (1985) also found that cross-sex friendships were ranked higher than romantic relationships on trust and acceptance. Finally, these researchers reported that casual and good cross-sex friendships were less stable than romantic relationships.

In addition to the above paradigm case formulations, only five studies have investigated how cross-sex friendships compare with romantic heterosexual relationships. The results of the earliest study, conducted by Rands and Levinger (1979), are difficult to interpret because the researchers investigated "good" same-sex and cross-sex friends, "close" same-sex and cross-sex relationships, and marital relationships. Therefore, because of the risk that the close cross-sex relationships may have been romantic in nature, one can only draw comparisons between "good" cross-sex friends and marital relationships. Not surprisingly, Rands and Levinger (1979) found good cross-sex friends ranked lower than marital relationships on both behavioral and affective interdependence.

A later study conducted by Argyle and Furnham (1983) expressly investigated close cross-sex friendships and marital relationships and thus provides specific information on the differences between these relational types. In this study, spouses scored higher, than cross-sex friends on the factors of satisfaction and conflict. The marital conflicts appeared to center on issues of independence while close cross-sex friends experienced conflict over a lack of understanding each other and an inability to discuss personal problems with one another.

Two studies researched the communication patterns of cross-sex friends and heterosexual romantic partners. First, Baxter and Wilmot (1984) identified taboo topics (topics that relational partners avoid discussing with one another) in platonic cross-sex relationships and in romantic couples. They found cross-sex friends had the lower number of taboo topics, whereas romantic couples had a higher number. For the overall sample, the taboo topic mentioned most by both groups was talk about the state of the relationship. However, romantic partners far outnumbered cross-sex friends in identifying this particular taboo topic.

Second, Baxter and Wilmot (1984) investigated the communication strategies used by cross-sex friends, romantic potential cross-sex dyads, and romantic heterosexual partners in order to gain information about the definition of their relationships. These researchers found that platonic cross-sex friends and romantic cross-sex partners utilized very few strategies to elicit information about the state of their relationship, while romantic potential cross-sex relational partners used a significantly greater number of such strategies.

Finally, I recently interviewed young adult women and men about their perceptions of the differences and similarities between their heterosexual romantic relationships and their cross-sex friendships (Werking, 1994a). These young adults identified many similarities between the two relational types. Specifically, they expected their romantic relationships and their opposite-sex friendships to involve a high level of trust, enjoyment, dependability, companionship, and understanding. Often, the participants described friendship as the basis for a romantic relationship. In other words, a romantic relationship was a friendship that involved "something more." One man summed up his feelings in the following way:

> "The two [cross-sex friendships and romantic relationships] are definitely similar in the fact that you like to do things, you like to share time together, you communicate, you open up to each other. Because I think the basis of a romantic relationship is that friendship, I think the romantic relationship is one step higher. I mean you have a wonderful friendship with that person, but you have these great feelings that puts it on a different level."

The most frequently mentioned characteristic of romantic relationships that differentiated them from cross-sex friendships was the physical attraction between romantic partners and the expression of that attraction. Many participants used this characteristic as the primary means of distinguishing between friendship and romance. A woman stated: "I think a romantic relationship happens when a guy kisses you or, you know, holds you a lot. That would probably be where the friendship ends and goes into something romantic." Similarly, a man said: "To me there's a difference between friends and a sexual partner. When you add a sexual part into a friendship, to me, it kinda ruins it."

Both men and women believed that cross-sex friends could be physically attracted to one another, but acting on that attraction transformed the friendship into a romantic pairing. In contrast, they maintained that physical attraction, whether acted upon or not, was necessary in the context of a romantic relationship.

The second characteristic distinguishing romantic relationships from opposite-sex friendships was the future orientation of romantic relationships. Men and women described their romantic partnerships as offering the possibility of monogamy, long-term commitment, or marriage. Because of these goals and the possibility of a physical union between romantic partners, men and women engaged in greater impression management with their romantic partners than with their cross-sex friends. According to one of the men, it appears that cross-sex friendship offers a freedom not found in romantic relationships:

"You can be yourself with your friend. In a dating relationship, you are trying to impress them. You always have . . . you don't want to do the wrong thing. With your friends, you can pretty much do . . . you're uninhibited with things with your opposite-sex friend. And that's how you can become . . . get closer with a friend like that."

The freedom found in a cross-sex friendship also involved fewer expectations about the friend's availability for activities. A woman described this type of freedom:

"You don't feel that they [cross-sex friends] are somebody you have to account to. In a romantic relationship, you know, there's that certain 'What are you doing?' In a friendship, you can just call them up and say, 'Hey, do you want to . . . ?' and not feel bad if they don't want to or if they have other plans or something."

Finally, the interviewees pointed to feelings in romantic relationships that were qualitatively different from those experienced in cross-sex friendships. In this area, the participants often had difficulty articulating these feelings, using such vague descriptors as a "special connection" or "magic." The following description was a typical response:

> "There's a special feeling between you and the person you are romantic with, the person that you care differently about. You can do everything with them intimately, but you also have that special feeling that's not there between you and your opposite-sex friend—some kind of special connection that makes you not just two people, but makes you one."

From these interviews, it seems that men and women do note differences as well as similarities between cross-sex friendships and romantic relationships. As one participant stated: "There's a fine line that separates them." For many persons the line between a friendship and a romantic relationship is most easily identified by the existence of a physical relationship between the relational partners. Other characteristics of romantic relationships, such as long-term goals of coupling and reduced freedom, are not found in cross-sex friendships.

The above characteristics identified during interviews mesh nicely with the results of survey data comparing friendship and the romantic relationship (e.g., Davis & Todd, 1985). Since cross-sex friendship *is* a form of friendship, we see clear differences in the goals and expectations of ideal/typical man–woman friendships and ideal/typical man–woman romantic relationships. Because of a lack of studies, however, we know few specifics about how these distinctions structure cross-sex friendships and romantic relationships.

Although the relational goals may differ for men and women engaged in friendships and those engaged in romantic relationships, in reality differences between the relational types may be lessened because of the overwhelming ideology of romantic love. In other words, men and women engaged in friendship with one another may succumb to the romantic ideology and begin to treat one another as potential romantic partners. Future comparative studies could, therefore, pinpoint how romantic ideology creeps into the enactment of man–woman friendships as well as how cross-sex friendships resist this ideology.

Given the paucity of existing research, more comparative studies are warranted. These studies should clearly define the type of cross-sex relationship under study since, as demonstrated by Rands and Levinger's (1979) study, a lack of clarity makes it difficult to interpret results. Clarity of definition would also ensure that investigators are researching platonic woman–man pairs rather than the friendship dimension of romantic or romantic-potential dyads.

ENACTING CROSS-SEX FRIENDSHIP IN AN AMBIGUOUS CULTURAL CONTEXT

Thus far, I have described how cross-sex friendship lies outside of two paradigmatic relationships. The positioning of cross-sex friendship in current middle-class American culture heightens the ambiguity surrounding how this form of relationship is defined and practiced. The ambiguity is increased by the manner in which cross-sex friendship is depicted in the media. A recent analysis of cross-sex friendship portrayals in film, television sitcoms, and the periodic literature from 1985 through 1993 (Werking, 1995) revealed a major finding: *cross-sex friendship is rarely seen in the media*. In contrast, participants in romantic relationships or in same-sex friendships are presented with extensive cultural images regarding the legitimate and desirable practice of their relationships since stories about romantic love saturate the media.

The absence of portrayals of cross-sex friendship reveals its marginal status in American society. As Rawlins (1993) states: "This relational category lacks its own master narrative in our culture" (p.53). Similarly, Ellin (1993) notes the ramifications of the lack of media models in citing the difficulties that men and women experience in establishing friendship across gender lines:

> Part of the problem may be a lack of role models depicting men and women as friends. With the exception of Huck Finn and Becky Thatcher, what other characters from books or films or the tube are strictly platonic friends? Harry and Sally ended up in bed; Sam and Diane thought things were through but, in fact, they weren't; *Moonlighting* went off the air as soon as Maddy and David started fooling around; and we all know what happened to Annie Hall. (p. 66)

Because of the material conditions surrounding the enactment of cross-sex friendship in middle-class American society, the establishment and maintenance of cross-sex friendship is *anomic* in nature. This anomie is perpetuated by the overwhelming influence of the ideology of romance and the failure of media programmers to consider cross-sex friendship as a legitimate topic.

Anomic situations are those for which society fails to provide clear guidelines. Since Durkheim, researchers of anomie have examined the consequences for individuals who find themselves in normless situations (Lampe, 1985). The consequences for individuals engaged in an anomic relationship include difficulty in both defining the relationship and interpreting their partner's behavior (Lampe, 1985). Similarly, observers of an anomic relationship cannot rely on socially specified guidelines for interpreting the relational partners' behaviors. As a result, such a relationship may be mislabeled or the partners may be looked upon as deviants by outsiders. For participants and observers, therefore, anomic relationships are potentially problematic.

As demonstrated in this chapter, confusion about appropriate behavior between male and female friends is one result of cross-sex friendship's position in the social structure. Because cross-sex friendship deviates from the norms associated with the romantic relationship, it has been called "an ambiguous relationship" (O'Meara, 1989), "anomalous" (Booth & Hess, 1974), "interfering" (Lopata, 1981), and open to labels of deviance (Rawlins, 1982).

Block (1980) sums up the status of cross-sex friendship in our society well when he states:

> Male–female ties—not bound by lover status or marriage—are rare and precarious; neither men nor women, for the most part, find them comfortable or easy to establish. . . . It is difficult to give up myths and old securities, to work out ways of relating that surmount sexual and sexist issues—the most common friendship complaints that men and women direct toward one another. (p. 105)

Block's comments highlight the difficulty that men and women experience when trying to transcend the ideology of romantic love. Friendship between women and men is often precarious because the institutionalization of romantic heterosexual love shapes what is "normal" behavior between women and men. Unfortunately, this ideology so permeates our thinking about woman–man relationships that it limits the possibilities for interaction across gender boundaries. For example, when faced with a novel situation—perhaps the possibility of a friendship with a member of the other sex—individuals tend to fall back on learned ways of thinking and continue to approach the other sex as if they were a potential romantic partner. This tendency may be particularly evident in developing cross-sex friendships or casual cross-sex friendships.

Studies support this notion since cross-sex friendships are seen as less stable (Davis & Todd, 1985) and shorter-lived than same-sex friendships (Parker & de Vries, 1993). Further, Rose (1985) reported that men often developed cross-sex friendships with hopes of redefining the friendship into a romantic relationship at a later date. Recognizing this tendency, women in this same study frequently stated that men's motives made them distrustful of male friendship overtures (Rose, 1985). Additional research in laboratory and field settings has found that women and men tend to interpret the friendly behavior of the other sex as an indication of sexual interest (Abbey, 1982, 1987). Finally, when men and women were questioned about why they did not have a close cross-sex friend, an often-mentioned response was that they regarded the opposite sex as potential lovers, not as potential friends (Werking, 1994b).

The dominance of the romantic ideology is maintained by denying the legitimacy of alternatives to the romantic heterosexual ideal or by subordinating those alternatives to the dominant philosophy. For instance, the legitimacy of cross-sex friendship is challenged by the popular saying "Men and women cannot be friends" and by its companion cultural debate over whether or not women and men *can* be friends. On the other hand, cross-sex friendship may be subsumed and, therefore, legitimated by the institution of romance by viewing cross-sex friendship merely as a stage in the development of a romantic relationship. Both strategies were evident in my analysis of media portrayals (Werking, 1995) since typical portrayals either viewed cross-sex friendship as a stepping-stone to romance or denied its existence by not placing it on the media agenda.

Scholars have also noted these strategies, exemplified by Swain

(1992) in his explanation of the messages that persons in developing cross-sex friendships receive from family members and friends. According to Swain, when a cross-sex friendship develops,

> family members and same-sex friends often tease, hint at, or praise the person for establishing a possible dating, sexual, or love relationship. Claims that "we're just good friends" are often viewed as withholding information, or as an indication of embarrassment or bashfulness about the sexual content of the relationship. (p. 154)

As indicated by Swain (1992), observers of a cross-sex friendship may not view the friendship as a legitimate relationship in its own right but may continue to view the relationship through the lens of romanticism—as an "undercover" romantic relationship. As a consequence, persons in fledgling cross-sex friendships are left with four alternatives: continue to insist that "we're only friends"; ignore the messages from outsiders; abandon the friendship; or, consistent with others' expectations, transform the friendship into a romantic relationship.

The dominance of romantic ideology in everyday life and in the media, coupled with the prevalence of friendships with members of the same-sex, contributes to the anomic quality of cross-sex friendship. This quality has been reflected in the words of persons whom I have interviewed about their close cross-sex friendships. These men and women acknowledged that their friendship was "abnormal," "a little strange," and "weird" and that "people don't understand it." The friends also commented that they did not have models of this type of friendship within their families, nor had their friends established many close cross-sex friends. Finally, when I asked them to describe cross-sex friendships that they had seen in the media, few of them could recall a media depiction of a cross-sex friendship that did not turn into a romantic relationship (the most commonly mentioned depiction was the film *When Harry Met Sally*). In short, these friends were quite aware that they were involved in a relationship that defied traditional expectations for man–woman relationships.

CONCLUSION

Cross-sex friendship's status in the present middle-class American culture and its mediated image in that culture influence the communicative management of these friendships since the interaction of cross-sex friends must surpass normative constraints and must reshape the way in which men and women typically interact with one another. The character of friendship allows for this transcendence, but in specific circumstances it may require that cross-sex friends do more "relational work" in actively managing both outside and inside concerns throughout the life of the friendship.

In a context where the societal practice of cross-sex friendship is not apparent, O'Meara (1989, 1994) and Rawlins (1982) posit that cross-sex friends must manage several challenges if their relationship is to endure. These challenges include (1) recreating ways of enacting friendship since men and women typically practice same-sex friendships differently; (2) overcoming the culturally sanctioned power differential between women and men; (3) negotiating the extent and meaning of romance and sexuality in the context of a platonic woman–man relationship; (4) presenting a legitimate image of cross-sex friendship to family, friends, coworkers, and acquaintances; and (5) carving out opportunities for the development of friendship. Failure to address these issues prohibits or threatens cross-sex friendship.

The men and women whom I have studied identified many of these issues when describing their own cross-sex friendship experiences and other issues important to the viability of their cross-sex friendships. In addition, several of these challenges are apparent in studies conducted by other researchers (e.g., Furman, 1986; Rawlins, 1981). The management of these challenges are the focus of the remaining chapters in this book. Therefore, I now turn to an analysis of the relational practices of cross-sex friends as they negotiate cross-sex friendship in an ambiguous societal climate.

2

■

The Private Side
of Cross-Sex Friendship I

Friendship Features and the Influence of Gender

TINA AND KEVIN

Tina, 22 years old, and Kevin, 24 years old, are East Indian, single, hetero-sexual, college students. They have been close friends for 1½ years.

Tina

What's special or unique about our friendship?

Kevin

Let's see.

Tina

Because he's so cute!

Kevin

Well, we have a lot of like inside jokes, and there are a lot of things that are funny. And when we're around other people, they'll like look at us and wonder. We have so many things that are confidential between us.

Tina

I think a lot of people wish they had as much fun as we do.

Kevin

Yeah, I know. When they're around us, they are just jealous that they're not like us or anything. What's unique about the friendship is, uh, if I want to go out and do something with somebody, anything especially adventurous or anything else, I know I can ask Tina to do it because . . .

Tina

Really? *(Laughs)*

Kevin

Really. 'Cause I know she'd want to do it and . . .

Tina

You better ask me!

Kevin

See? If I don't ask her, that's what'll happen! So, I can usually rely on her to do stuff for the most part, more than any other girl probably or more than almost any other friend.

Tina

It's not that I have fun with you all the time. We always have fun together, except for those tension moments that we have. But we can just sit there and talk about anything personal. We never really talk about each other's family, but just personal stuff—school, what century you're graduating . . .

Kevin

Yeah, I predict 21st century.

Tina

. . . gossiping about our friends, what's up with everyone. That's cool because he knows pretty much all the people I know. Um, he knows where I'm coming from.

Kevin

Yeah.

As I have argued in earlier chapters in this book and elsewhere (Werking, 1996), researchers largely have dismissed cross-sex friendship as a legitimate research topic. In addition, in the instances when the topic is studied, research has focused on discovering the affective nature of cross-sex friendship. Thus, other basic features of cross-sex friendship—such as the content of talk and the activities of cross-sex friends—have been minimally investigated by other researchers. Given the current state of the field, and in the hope of sparking future research, I must rely on the results of my own studies into each of these areas while describing these features in the following sections. I provide details of these studies in the appendices so that the reader may judge the usefulness of my results. In the final section of this chapter, I will describe the influence of gender on the character of cross-sex friendship, reviewing the research of other scholars as well as my own.

CROSS-SEX FRIENDS' ACTIVITIES AND TOPICS OF TALK

In the conversation at the beginning of this chapter, Tina and Kevin talk about how important it is to their friendship that they do many activities together and talk with one another about important personal matters. What activities do cross-sex friends enjoy together? What do cross-sex friends talk about together? This chapter provides some answers to these questions, although the amount of information regarding these areas is limited. The activities of cross-sex friends will be described prior to a consideration of the content of their conversations.

My interviews with cross-sex friends as well as a survey that I recently conducted (Werking, 1994d) have garnered information about what cross-sex friends do together. These studies utilized different methodologies, however, their findings are quite similar. First, during in-depth interviews with pairs of friends, cross-sex friends said they rent movies, dine, shop, drive around, play cards, walk, ride bicycles, and work out. Second, a survey of 170 young adults involved in a close cross-sex friendship revealed that in the month prior to the study the things that they did together were to eat meals at home and in restaurants, watch television, visit friends, go for walks or drives, and shop (Werking, 1994d).

The primary friendship activity of cross-sex friends in both studies, however, was talking together. The most frequently reported activities in the survey were discussing personal issues (73.2% of the sample), talking on the phone (70.8%), eating a meal (67.9%), discussing nonpersonal issues (67.3%), and going to a restaurant (59.5%). In the majority of the conversations between cross-sex friends, the partners talked with each other without the participation of anyone else. Thus, it appears that cross-sex friends enjoy talking with one another and engage in activities, such as sharing a meal together, that facilitate conversation.

These findings are also apparent in interviews, where, over and over again, men and women have responded to my question, "What do you typically do when you are together?" by stating, "We sit and talk." These friends tell each other stories about their lives and talk about their problems and their relationships. Friends share their experiences so that they can better understand each other's lives. During interview after interview, I heard that one of the most valuable components of a close cross-sex friendship was the opportunity to begin to make sense of the opposite sex and to apply that understanding to one's own situation.

I also asked my interviewees about the sorts of topics that they usually discuss with their cross-sex friend. From their answers it appeared that these friends were exceptionally open with one another, examining through conversation their feelings and personal experiences on a regular basis. This openness is illustrated in the following excerpt from an interview with Carl and Anne.

Interviewer

What sorts of things do you talk about?

Anne

We talk about everything! *(Both laugh)* There's really . . . there's nothing that's off limits!

Carl

No.

Anne

Cause we have conversations where we just . . .

Carl

. . . about sex or lack thereof.

Anne

I was goin' to say that we have conversations *(laughing)* that are, like, fun . . . happy conversations. But then we also talk about life.

Carl

Yeah, anything from, like, family trouble or, like, music. There's such a broad range.

Anne

Yeah.

Interviewer

What do you like most about your friendship?

Anne

That I can talk to him about anything, and that we can have fun.

Carl

Mm hmm. Always, doin' anything. We could, like, knit, and have fun! *(All laugh)*

Anne

And I always feel safe with Carl 'cause I know that no matter what, he's always going to be there for me and make me feel better. And just what we said before, there's nothing we can't talk about.

Carl

That's true.

A broad range of conversational topics was also evident in the survey cited above (Werking, 1994d). This survey asked persons to provide information about topics that they discuss with their close cross-sex friends as well as topics that they avoid talking about with their friends. The results indicate that the friends' personal lives constitute a great portion of their conversational topics (see Table 2.1).

Few topics were actively avoided by these friends, and the percentages for such topics are small (see Table 2.2).

TABLE 2.1. Most Frequently Reported Conversational Topics of Close Cross-Sex Friends

Topic	Percentage of sample reporting topic
Friends	84.5
Future—goals, plans	78.0
Personal problems	77.4
Daily activities	76.8
Stressors	72.0
Work	70.8
School	64.9
Mutual activities	64.3
Romantic partners	60.7
Reminisce about past	55.4

Discussing feelings for one another was the most frequently reported taboo topic. Since this topic is actively avoided by friends, it appears that keeping silent about feelings is one strategy for preserving the friendship. A sampling of the reasons that this topic was avoided follows:

"It is hard for me to communicate about my deepest feelings concerning someone close to me." *(Man, 23 years old)*

"We are not romantically involved. However, there has been several points in our relationship in which he has been "interested" in me, wanting more than a friend. This hurt our relationship because I am not able to deal with his feeling this way about me. We fought about this many times. As a result, we do not openly discuss our

TABLE 2.2. Most Frequently Reported Taboo Conversational Topics of Close Cross-Sex Friends

Topic	Percentage of sample reporting topic
Feelings about friend	32.7
Politics	29.8
Religion	26.8
Personal flaws	20.2
Family problems	13.7

relationship and our feelings about each other. Although we don't talk about it, we both know that we care about each other and we support each other." *(Woman, 19 years old)*

"We used to date and never really resolved our feelings for each other." *(Man, 26 years old)*

"There is no point in talking about this subject because it's understood that we are great friends. Why talk about it?" *(Man, 25 years old)*

"At one time he wanted to be more than friends. I didn't and wouldn't ever, so we avoid that topic." *(Woman, 21 years old)*

Although there has been limited study of the activities and content of the talk of close cross-sex friends, the existing studies strongly suggest that cross-sex friends discuss with one another personal matters such as problems, future plans, and work or school issues. Further, it appears that cross-sex friends' relationships with others—romantic partners, family, coworkers, and other friends—constitute a substantial portion of their talk. Since I will describe this type of cross-sex friendship talk in my discussion of cross-sex friends' relationships with third parties in Chapter 5, I will not offer specifics at this time.

The results of these studies are most closely aligned with the findings of studies that have investigated the talk of female friends (Aries & Johnson, 1983; Davidson & Duberman, 1982; Johnson & Aries, 1983). These studies found that female friends tend to talk about a wide variety of topics, ranging from personal and relational matters to impersonal topics, while male friends tend to restrict their conversational content to more impersonal topics. Further, in these studies men did not place as much emphasis on talk in their friendship as women did, although for both male and female friends conversation constituted an important same-sex friendship activity.

The point I want to emphasize here is that close cross-sex friends do tend to develop an emotionally supportive dyad that is evident in the activities that they do together and in the content of their talk. This support system is valued by both men and women, who expressed a strong dependency on the friendship during their interviews:

"I need his friendship. I really have to have it. And he knows I miss him. He knows I love him. And he knows I need him. But I don't think he has any idea how much I need his friendship." *(Woman, 37 years old)*

"I don't have any brothers and sisters, but it's kind of like that. Where would you be? It's hard to imagine things without her, you know, because every now and then it's like, you know, I've gotta hear that laugh that she does. That cheesiness, you know. I've just gotta hear that. It's like craving your favorite food or something." *(Man, 24 years old)*

The closeness of these bonds was also apparent when I questioned cross-sex friends about how they demonstrate their commitment to their friendship. Their responses usually centered around "making time" for the friendship. The men and women whom I interviewed led very active lives, and so "making time" for a friend was seen as a way of letting a friend know that one was willing to sacrifice other interests for the friendship. Many of these friends were separated geographically, and taking the time to write letters, make phone calls, or schedule visits with a friend was also viewed as an expression of commitment.

The close cross-sex friends whom I interviewed also discussed their affection for one another, both verbal and nonverbal. Physical touching was permissible in many of the friendships. Consequently, cross-sex friends described hugging, kissing, rubbing each other's backs, and linking arms as natural expressions of affection. For the majority of my interviewees, their primary interpretation of physical contact was that it expressed affection and not hidden sexual desire. In the next chapter, as I focus on the management of romance and sexuality in cross-sex friendship, I will discuss how these interpretations developed.

In sum, little information is available on the activities and conversations of cross-sex friends. By and large, researchers have concentrated heavily on documenting the influence of gender on the affective character of cross-sex friendship. A primary focus of same-sex friendship research has been on the relationship between gender and friendship characteristics; therefore, it appears that this interest has carried over into the context of cross-sex friendship. In fact, most of the information about the role of gender in cross-sex friendship comes from research in which the relations between gender, same-sex friendship, and cross-sex friendship are compared within the same study. I adopt this design for my discussion as I first describe the nature of same-sex friendships of women and men and then review studies that have compared the perceptions that women and men have of cross-sex friendship.

The following descriptions attempt to capture many of the characteristics of same-sex and cross-sex friendships of men and women that have been identified in the existing literature. The differences between the friendship styles of men and women, however, should not be overdrawn since evidence from studies employing within-gender as well as between-gender analyses suggests that these differences are small and that many similarities in the friendship styles of women and men exist as well (e.g., Burleson, Kunkel, Samter, & Werking, 1996; Duck & Wright, 1993; Monsour, 1992). At the end of this chapter, I revisit this issue and incorporate the findings from my interviews into the current debate about the role of gender in the enactment of friendship.

THE ROLE OF GENDER IN CROSS-SEX AND SAME-SEX FRIENDSHIP

Researchers have argued that men and women enact same-sex friendships in distinct ways, although men and women share similar conceptions of the ideal friendship. Specifically, adult female friendships have been called "communal" in nature (Bakan, 1966) because of the recurrent finding that women's same-sex friendships tend to involve higher levels of emotional expression. The expressivity of women's same-sex friendship is found in adolescent girls' friendships (Youniss & Smollar, 1985) and continues throughout the young adult years (Rawlins, 1992). Talk is a salient activity for female friends. Talk among women weaves a "mosaic" of emotions, feelings, and support (Johnson & Aries, 1983). The interweaving of lives is reflected in women's topics of talk since, typically, female friends are more apt than male friends to discuss with greater frequency, reciprocity, and depth personal problems, intimate relationships, and feelings (Aries & Johnson, 1983; Parker & de Vries, 1993). Perhaps as a result, women report an enhancement of self-worth because of their friendships (Johnson & Aries, 1983). Female friends, in general, are also more apt to attempt to work through conflicts or problems in their relationships. This inclination is reported in adolescent friendships (Youniss & Smollar, 1985) as well as in adult friendships (Weiss & Lowenthal, 1975).

Adult male friendships have been described as "agentic" (Bakan, 1966) in character. In general, men consistently report that doing activities with their friends, such as participating in sports, is an important component of their same-sex friendships (Caldwell & Peplau, 1982). However, for most men, talk does not seem to be as salient an activity as it is for female friends. Male topics of talk also seem to differ, reflecting their friendship world of shared activities. Typically, men report discussing sports and mutually shared activities more frequently than women do. Though men also report sharing personal feelings and problems, in general they do not share these aspects of their lives as frequently or as revealingly as women do (Aries & Johnson, 1983). Male same-sex friends also appear to handle problems in their friendships differently from the ways in which women do since men are more reluctant to confront male friends about bothersome attitudes or behaviors (Youniss & Smollar, 1985).

Given these gender-related styles of friendship, one of the challenges facing men and women in friendship with one another may be shedding friendship expectations and behaviors learned in the context of same-sex friendship and learning alternative ways of practicing friendship. Thus far, most research in this area has focused on examining the effect of respondents' sex on the reported affective character of their cross-sex friendships and same-sex friendships, drawing comparisions between the friendship types. As a result, I will examine separately male and female perspectives on cross-sex and same-sex friendship.

When asked to describe their friends, most men draw clear distinctions between their male friends and their female friends. Men usually describe their female friends as "imaginative," "abstract," "relaxed," "happy-go-lucky," and "venturesome" (Mahoney & Heretick, 1979). In contrast, most men describe their male friends in terms of physical and cognitive rivalry, using such descriptors as "willpower," "assertiveness," and "leadership" (Mahoney & Heretick, 1979). The competitive element of male–male friendship has been discussed in numerous studies examining gender differences in same-sex friendship (e.g., Reisman, 1981; Weiss & Lowenthal, 1975). It would appear that cross-sex friendship offers men relief from this competitiveness since males report experiencing more nurturing, intimacy, and enjoyment (Sapadin, 1988); emotional support (Aukett et al., 1988; Rubin, 1985); caring and acceptance (Sapadin, 1988); and security (Furman, 1986) from their female friends than from their male friends. Resembling the above surveys, Bell's (1981b) interviews reveal that, generally, men attribute feelings of love, affection, and warmth to their cross-sex friends and that these feelings are not usually attributed to their male friends.

In comparison, women tend to describe a more ambivalent view of their friendships with males. Women are less likely to name a man as a close friend than men are to name a woman as a close friend (Rose, 1985). Rubin (1985) reported that approximately two-thirds of the women named by a man as a close friend did not agree with that definition. These women acknowledged a friendship with the man, but did not categorize it as a close one. The following results of studies lend insight into why these women might hesitate to label their cross-sex friendships as "close" in nature.

First, women are more apt to discuss their personal problems with their female friends than with their male friends (Aukett et al., 1989). Perhaps that is why women, in general, report receiving more therapeutic support (Aukett et al., 1988) and a greater degree of self-affirmation (Furman, 1986) from their friendships with women. Rose (1985) also observes that women perceived their cross-sex friendships as less intimate and accepting than their same-sex friendships. Furman (1986) indicates that some women in her study experienced a "lesser sense of the personal" with their male friends (p. 112). These disparities may be due to the different ways in which, according to some authors, men and women approach their social worlds. As a group, women seem to value the process of talking through a problem or analyzing relationships and events with one another (Aries & Johnson, 1983; Gilligan, 1982).

Although women typically perceive their friendships with men as less intimate than their close female friendships, women seem to enjoy the companionship provided by cross-sex friendship since they tend to report higher levels of companionship in their cross-sex friendships than in their same-sex friendships (Rose, 1985). The "cooler ambience" (Rubin, 1985) of cross-sex friendship may offer women, in general, sanctuary from the difficulties inherent in managing a close female–female friendship. For example, as a group, females experience higher levels of conflict in their same-sex friendships (Wright, 1982). Women also report that they can take and give criticism more easily with their male friends than with their female friends (Rubin, 1985). Because of the affectively charged character of same-sex friendship, most women perceive their same-sex friendships as more difficult to maintain than their cross-sex friendships.

Apparently, men and women perceive their friendships with one another in somewhat different ways. Men as a group tend to view cross-sex friendship as a nurturing and intimate relationship in which they may express their feelings. Women, on the other hand, typically view cross-sex friendship as less personal and mutually disclosive but enjoy the companionship offered by this type of friendship.

Yet, despite these contrasting perceptions, comparative studies also find many similarities in the descriptions by men and women. First, for both sexes, cross-sex friendship tends to provide new understandings and perceptions of the other sex (Sapadin, 1988). Sapadin (1988) found that the responses from both men and women to her interview question, "What do you like most about your cross-sex friendships?" tended to be that they gained new insights into the other sex's perspective. It appears that exposure to these dissimilarities in the context of friendship may help men and women to find different ways to approach and solve problems. Second, there was similarity between sexes in the reported amount of intimacy and enjoyment (Monsour, 1992; Sapadin, 1988) and in the functions of help, availability, and recognition in cross-sex friendship (Rose, 1985). Third, as I will discuss in more detail in Chapter 5, both men and women tend to keep their friendships and sexual relationships separate (Sapadin, 1988). Finally, for both sexes, opening up to another perspective may also result in a rethinking of values and beliefs (Furman, 1986).

In Chapter 1, I noted that the ideal conceptions of men and women about cross-sex friendship resemble their ideal conceptions of same-sex friendships. It is possible, however, that these ideal images of friendship fail to reflect the realities of enacting the two different forms of friendship. For example, past studies, because of their reliance on the survey method, provide limited specific information about the nature of gender-related behaviors in the enactment of same- and cross-sex friendships.

For these reasons, I questioned women and men extensively about how their actual experiences of close cross-sex friendships corresponded with their experiences of close same-sex friendships. During these interviews, I heard how the enactments of close same-sex and close cross-sex friendships diverge in actual practice. I also gained greater insight into the role of gender in these deviations.

ACTUAL EXPERIENCES OF CLOSE CROSS-SEX AND SAME-SEX FRIENDSHIP

Overall, the described experiences of same-sex friendships for my interviewees correlated with existing same-sex friendship research findings reviewed previously. Specifically, the men reported that their same-sex friendships primarily involved doing activities, such as drinking together, playing sports, and hunting. Further, though the men did report talking with their male friends about a variety of things, they did not discuss personal problems or feelings in much depth. It should be noted that a small number of my male interviewees did describe close same-sex friendships in which they consistently shared quite personal concerns with one another. Interestingly, however, these men also recognized and indicated that these friendships deviated from their usual friendships with men.

Also paralleling the same-sex friendship literature, the female interviewees portrayed their close same-sex friendships as relationships in which they shared much of themselves—talking about relationships, problems, feelings, and "gossiping" with one another. They also stated that their same-sex friendships were often filled with strife. One theme that has emerged in these interviews and that has not received much previous research attention is the competition that arises between female friends. This theme has been frequently mentioned and seems to be one of the least-liked aspects of female–female friendship.

When I inquired about the sources of competition between female friends, women mentioned "men," "clothes," "monetary things," "looks," "lifestyles," "weight," and "credit cards." Melanie summed up her feelings regarding this theme in female same-sex friendships: "I think if we [women] let each other bond to each other and be real friends to each other, I think we would have a little more understanding of each other." Referring to bonding, Melanie said:

"I don't think we do. Because women always compete. For men, for whatever. For cheerleading. For, you know . . . we're always in competition *with each other*. Men compete, but they join a team and compete together against this outside force. And we aren't taught that. I hope girls are being better taught now."

The women's annoyance with this element of female friendship was one reason cited for enjoying their friendships with men. In short, they did not compete with their male friends and were relieved not to do so.

Not surprisingly, the general pattern of these descriptions of same-sex friendships suggests that the male and female participants in my interviews have developed dissimilar same-sex friendship styles although they share similar conceptions of the ideal friendship. The role of gender becomes more complex, however, when the behavior of men and women in same-sex friendships is compared with their behavior in cross-sex friendships. That is, the close cross-sex friends whom I interviewed provided data that suggest a fluidity of male and female behavior when interacting across gender boundaries.

For both men and women, I noted differences and similarities in their behavior in cross-sex friendships, as compared with their behavior in the context of same-sex friendships. In order to demonstrate this behavioral mutability and flexibility, I turn now to men's accounts of the differences and similarities between their close same-sex friendships and their close friendships with women. Then, I address women's comparisons of their close same-sex and cross-sex friendships.

Men's Comparisons of Close Same-Sex and Cross-Sex Friendships

The men whom I interviewed pointed out many differences and few similarities between their close same-sex friendships and their close cross-sex friendships. The theme of difference in these descriptions is typified in one male's answer to my question, "How are your close friendships with women similar to your close friendships with men?" He responded, "How are they *similar*? Gosh, they aren't!" By and large, the men described differences generally centered around the type of talk found in male–male dyads and male–female dyads. As these men described their friendships with other men, they repeatedly talked about how males were "stuck in the macho-type thing" or were concerned with playing the masculine role with their male friends. One man commented that men construct "walls that are too thick." Another man said that men were more inclined to keep with the "manhood side of themselves rather than their heart." The roles that men play appear to shape the character of male–male friendships and are further perpetuated by these friendships. The men whom I interviewed stated that they talked with male friends about a variety of things, such as work, play, and personal situations, but that none of these topics were discussed in much depth or with much emotion.

When they talked about their male friendships, I did not get the impression that these men were necessarily dissatisfied with their male friendships, although a small number of the men openly criticized the lack of intimacy in male friendships. Ironically, the limited dissatisfaction that they expressed seemed to stem from the close correspondence between their expectations of male friendship and their actual experiences with male friends. They realized that their male friends could be dependable and fun companions, but would not necessarily offer much emotional support. So, instead of expecting such support from their close male friends, they turned to their close female friends.

Since I was intrigued by the clear distinction that they drew between their same-sex and their cross-sex friendships, I asked the men why they were better able to talk to female friends than male friends about personal matters. Their responses to my questions focused on the idea that women exhibit sensitivity and concern for others and that these qualities enabled the men to feel comfortable about sharing personal concerns. Roy and I discussed this issue at length. When I asked, "How would you compare your close friendships with females with your close male friendships?" he responded:

"Well, in some strange ways they're closer than with males. Because females tend to be more open and talk more about things than men, and that's a natural phenomenon. So, in some ways you end up talking to them more about things.

"They are not too different in terms of the topics you talk about or the breadth of it. I can think of two males that I'm very close friends with, and we talk about work, we talk about better lives, we talk about, in one case, his wife and his kids and that kind of stuff. The level of conversation is different because it's a man versus a female. But with Phyl sometimes it's more emotional, more thought provoking or introspective than with the males. Males tend to be more rational and factual. 'Here's the problem, here's the alternatives, let's pick one. Okay, fine, let's go on to the next thing.'

"Women tend to be more caring than men in a relationship. So when you're really hurting or when you're down in the dumps, they tend to pay more attention to you."

Peter discussed a different relational dynamic that distinguished his close friendship with Laura from his close friendships with men:

"She's not macho. She, uh . . . my guard is never up with her. Um, where with most of my male friends it seems like that's the way it is now. And, uh, she's not competitive with me. It seems like one of the biggest obstacles in a lot of my other friendships is just the competitiveness. Men are . . . men suck. They're just always trying to beat each other over the head and shit. I just hate it."

The other men in my sample utilized words similar to Roy's and Peter's when describing their female friends. Words such as "receptive," "personal," "nurturing," and "emotional" were quite evident in their narratives. And as Roy stated, becoming friends with a person who exhibits those qualities changes the character of the talk of friends and thus provides the opportunity for reciprocated nurturance.

These activities of cross-sex friends' were also different from the activities that men typically pursue with their same-sex friends. As I mentioned previously, men's same-sex friends were involved in playing competitive sports, hunting, drinking, and being, as one man observed, "rude and crazy" together. On the whole, these types of activities were not shared by the cross-sex friends.

Instead, their primary friendship activity was talking. Through this talk, men felt free to express both positive and negative emotion and to demonstrate affection by verbal and nonverbal means. Negotiating this type of friendship appears to differ not only from developing the normative male–male friendship bond reported in the research literature but also from the close same-sex friendship experiences of men described to me.

Women's Comparisons of Close Same-Sex and Cross-Sex Friendships

The women whom I interviewed presented a different picture of their same-sex and cross-sex friendships. Their comparisons diverge somewhat from the men's viewpoint; for although the men whom I interviewed clearly differentiated between the levels of emotionality in their same-sex friendships and cross-sex friendships, the women were less inclined to note differences.

The primary theme when comparing men's close same-sex and cross-sex friendships was one of difference. In contrast, the main theme evidenced by the women whom I interviewed was one of similarity between the emotional web woven in their close friendships with other women and in their close friendships with men. A woman commented on this likeness by saying that cross-sex and same-sex friendships were "similar in that we . . . we like the same things and we talk about problems, about our feelings to one another."

Unlike the suggestion made by Bernard (1986) and Rose (1985) that females experience "social deprivation" in their friendships with men, these women appeared to enjoy reciprocated personalism in their close cross-sex friendships. For example, these words belie the claim of social deprivation:

"With Bryan sometimes, you know, there can be . . . there can be lows. We talk about the things that hurt me and stuff like that. You know, sometimes it's really fun and it's really high and exciting with Bryan, and then sometimes it's really low. Because I think that we're so close that we feel each other's pain, you know, and that's the hardest thing, the hardest thing. Because when he's down, I'm down, and I think when I'm down, he's down too."

In fact, not one female friend whom I interviewed expressed dissatisfaction with the degree of reciprocated affect in her close cross-sex friendship. On the contrary, the majority of these women stated that their relationships with their male friends involved a degree of confidentiality, trustworthiness, honesty, dependability, and intimacy that equaled or in some cases surpassed that found in their close female friendships.

In addition to the similarity between the degree of affect in their cross-sex and same-sex friendships, these women also described engaging in the same types of activities with their male friends as with their female friends. This overlap is not surprising since, as I stated previously, the primary cross-sex friendship activity of these participants was talking, and talking with their female friends is also very important to these women. One difference between their activities with female friends and male friends was in the area of alcohol and narcotic consumption. Several women did state that they go to bars with their male friends more than with their female friends and were more apt to smoke marijuana with their male friends.

Even though there were strong similarities between the women's perceptions of same-sex and cross-sex friendships, there were notable differences in their experiences, namely, in the area of relational problematics. In the past, these women had experienced difficulties with their female friends. These difficulties included breaches of confidentiality, undependability, and neglect of the friendship because of a romantic interest in a man. In addition, as I pointed out previously, the women spoke quite strongly about their dissatisfaction with the competitive element of female friendships. It appears that, at times, this competition and the difficulties listed above influenced the women's willingness to be vulnerable with their female friends. As a result, these women were more apt to turn to their close male friends when they were in need of support. The following are some of the women's remarks regarding these problems:

> "I feel as though I can trust them [males] more than I can another girl, probably. Girls you always think flap their jaws and tell everything that they know. And guys are much more confidential. They stay to themselves."

> "[Males are] usually closer friends. Like in the same sex I kind of feel jealousy, can sense jealousy a lot of times with girls. And with guys, I don't feel that."

> "Sometimes, um, I could trust a man in a way that, um, I could think like, well, as a female they're going to think automatically in terms of the female's point of view. And a male point of view I can trust them to be honest—to be honest with me and not worry about my feelings as much as just to make sure that I'm on the right path. So I think they're more . . . I think it would be honest."

It was apparent in their comments that the women whom I interviewed valued their friendships with other women but were well aware of the possibilities for difficult relational dynamics. It seems that in a relational context in which gender identity is heightened, emotional interdependency functions differently than it does in a context in which it may be less salient, as in women's close cross-sex friendships. The influence of the relational context was also noted in the men's same-sex friendships where the men reported enacting stereotypical male gender identity with their male friends while also describing nonstereotypical behavior with their female friends.

Even with the potential for discord, however, there were situations in which these women specifically sought out the support of female friends. These situations, such as needing to talk about marriage or children, are those in which talking with a person who has a similar set of life experiences is preferred. In other words, in these situations, gender is highly salient because of its associated set of experiences. Although obtaining the perspective of the opposite sex is considered to be extremely valuable in some circumstances, it appears at other times that the empathy generated from the shared female experience is very beneficial.

According to these women, their close friendships with males provided an attractive alternative to close same-sex friendships. Meanwhile, their close cross-sex friendships shared several important characteristics of their friendships with other women. Specifically, as with their close same-sex friendships, these females enjoyed a high degree of emotional interdependency, participated in similar activities, and were able to talk about a wide range of topics with their close cross-sex friends. Further, cross-sex friendships became more attractive because the women did not experience many of the problems with their close male friends that they experienced with their close female friends. In fact, few problems within these cross-sex friendships were cited. The problems that were discussed primarily resulted from managing their friendships in the context of their other relationships, such as romantic relationships, family relationships, and other friendships. I will address these problematics in depth in Chapter 5.

The Role of Gender: Summary

In conclusion, for the men, experiencing close friendships with women was distinct from their experiences of close friendships with men. Cross-sex friendships provided an opportunity for men to explore and cultivate a different friendship style, one that was emotionally involving and centered on the intimate sharing of self. Focusing exclusively on male behavior in the context of same-sex friendship has led some researchers to posit that males act in shallow or incompetent ways as friends and has led researchers to question whether males have the ability to form intimate friendships (e.g., Bell, 1981b; Fasteau, 1975). In formulating these speculations, researchers have looked only at men's abilities to act in particular ways in one type of friendship context. Unfortunately, how specific relational contexts influence these abilities has not been considered fully. Comparing these males' reported behavior in their close cross-sex friendships with their behaviors in their close same-sex friendships increases the complexity of our understanding of men's practices as friends and clearly demonstrates the need for further consideration of diverse relational contexts.

As with my analysis of men's behavior in differing friendship contexts, examining women's reported behavior in their close same-sex and cross-sex friendships further enriches our understanding of the role of gender-related practices in friendship. For these women also demonstrated fluidity in their friendship behavior depending on the relational context, although not to the same degree as the men whom I interviewed.

From the perspective of these females, close cross-sex friendships closely approximated their intimate friendships with other women. The most striking similarity with their female friendships they discussed centered on the salience and quality of talk and in the degree of emotional interdependency achieved through that talk. Still, there were differences in the behaviors of these women in their close same-sex and close cross-sex friendships. It appears that, for these women, same-sex friendship was a context in which their gender identities were heightened as they interacted woman to woman. One manifestation of this emphasis was women's competing against one another about gender-typical matters. Because the tension of managing this type of competition was not present in their cross-sex friendships, these women were willing to be more emotionally involved with their male friends.

My analysis of these data has revealed many similarities between the behaviors of men and women in the context of cross-sex friendship. Too often men and women are viewed as being "qualitatively and permanently different" (Thorne, 1986. p. 168) in their enactments of friendship (see also Wright, 1988). Much of this thinking is a result of an almost exclusive focus on same-sex friendship and a zealous search for difference in behavior. As a result, we know little about how men and women interact across gender boundaries in friendship. Nor do we know much about the similarities between male and female behavior in either same-sex friendship or in cross-sex friendship.

As indicated by my interviewees, gender-related practices are altered when men and women interact across gender boundaries in a relationship that is not defined as romantic or sexual in nature. In a relationship not infused with heterosexual meanings (Thorne, 1986), gender identity seems to be less salient. Variations in behavior are possible and even facilitated that are not found in situations where gender identity is heightened, as in same-sex friendships and romantic heterosexual relationships.

These interviews, however, only present data about man–woman friendships that are close in nature and have minimal romantic or sexual undertones. In fact, the specific definitions that I set forth regarding the type and closeness of the friendships that I wanted to study may explain the discrepancies in the results of my interviews and in the studies reviewed above that found that women rated their cross-sex friendships as less close in nature. Several of the studies reviewed in this chapter have not clearly defined cross-sex friendship as a nonromantic relationship between a woman and a man (e.g., Bell, 1981a; Kamorovsky, 1974; Rubin, 1985) or have not assessed the level of closeness experienced in the friendship (e.g., Block, 1980; Bukowski et al., 1988; Furman, 1986). Therefore, it is possible that participants in other studies may have reported on casual cross-sex friendships or on cross-sex relationships that may have been romantic-potential or dating relationships. This possibility has ramifications for research results because in friendships permeated with romantic or sexual meanings or in those that are more casual in nature the behavior of men and women may vary from those persons participating in platonic, close relationships.

CONCLUSION

This chapter has explored many of the basic features of cross-sex friendship. Even so, there are many unanswered research questions. A sampling of these questions includes the following: What types of ritualized interaction occur in cross-sex friendships? How do these friendship rituals evolve? How do conversational topics become taboo in cross-sex friendships? How do personal topics get talked about by cross-sex friends? How do cross-sex friends mutually solve problems? Obviously, this list of questions merely scratches the surface, and interested researchers can look forward to investigating the dynamics of cross-sex friendship for many years to come.

The topic of the perceptions of cross-sex friendship by men and women has been more thoroughly investigated than the above research areas. Yet, most of these investigations have limited themselves simply to gathering both sexes' perceptions of the affective characteristics of cross-sex friendship. I encourage researchers to delve into other issues as well, such as power relations between cross-sex friends, everyday interactions, and the meanings that behaviors hold for friends. Such investigations should strive for a deeper understanding of cross-sex friendship and should search for similarities as well as differences between female and male descriptions of these relational issues.

3

The Private Side of Cross-Sex Friendship II

Opportunities for Development and Continuance

TOM AND PERRI

Perri, 34 years old, is white, a college graduate, and married. Tom, 34 years old, is white, a college graduate, homosexual, and is in a committed relationship. Tom and Perri have been close friends for 15 years.

Tom

> Sue [Perri's sister] was sort of a magnet. That's how we got together in a way. We went cruisin' and went to Sue's.

Perri

> Yeah, yeah. Because that's where we could go. You're right. Oh, Tom, you've got such a way with words! *(Pause)* I think we went through a spell when you were workin' at Stryker and I was living . . . remember when Mom and Bob got divorced and I was living at home? We leaned on each other a lot during that time.

Tom

> Yeah.

Perri

> I think we did. Everything was geared around, "Well, what's Tom doin'? Well, I can't do that 'cause Tom can't . . ."

Tom

It's hard for me to think back. I've been, you know, so many places and it's like . . .

Perri

That's true. But I remember you riding your bicycle and I had to be home at 11 o'clock.

Tom

Yeah. That was freshman year—summer. But then, when did you move to Frankfort?

Perri

Uh, I moved in, uh, fall of '79.

Tom

So, we must have had the summer of '79, and then you moved.

Perri

Yeah, and then I moved, and you came to Frankfort.

Tom

Yeah, and then I . . . well, then you began with Michael. And then I sort of stayed at home and hung out with Sue.

Perri

Right. Yeah, you became . . . I was jealous.

Tom

Really?

Perri

Yes, I was. I was jealous you spent more time with Sue.

Tom

Yeah, but you were just beginning a relationship, too.

Perri

I know, but that bothered me! 'Cause I was trying to figure out how to juggle the two relationships. They were two different relationships, but I was extremely jealous that you were spending a lot of time with Sue!

In the past, the structure of the social activities of men and women (McCall, 1988) provided little opportunity for them to initiate and maintain friendships with one another. In other words, "opportunity structures" (O'Meara, 1994, p.4) for the development and maintenance of cross-sex friendship were not in force. Opportunity structures are configurations of physical settings, personal predispositions, and social forces that encourage or obstruct relationship development and sustenance. For example, an opportunity structure for cross-sex friendship development facilitates sustained contact between men and women of equal status in a supportive normative environment (O'Meara, 1994). While O'Meara (1994) focused on the opportunity structures for the development of cross-sex friendship, I extend his concept to encompass the continuance of cross-sex friendship as well since the above configurations impinge on friendships throughout people's lives.

Although the rigid social norms guiding man–woman interaction have become more flexible, the opportunities for the development of cross-sex friendship may continue to be limited. In fact, O'Meara (1994) maintains that adults continue to face a "cross-sex friendship opportunity challenge" (p. 4). That is, he contends that the contexts and structures of the lives of men and women may continue to deter cross-sex friendship opportunities.

As illustrated in Perri and Tom's conversation, several factors, such as proximity, stressors emanating from family relationships, and commitments to other relationships, shape the character of cross-sex friendship. This chapter, therefore, describes the structures in the lives of men and women that may facilitate or impede the development and continuance of cross-sex friendship.

First, I will review the cross-sex friendship literature in order to ascertain what structural characteristics have been found to affect the development and nature of cross-sex friendship. Second, I will describe how the men and women whom I have interviewed became, and continued to be, close friends. Third, we can learn about the opportunities for the development of cross-sex friendship by studying persons who do not have cross-sex friends as well as those who do. Therefore, I will report the results of a survey of men and women who did not have close cross-sex friendships at the time of the study. Finally, impediments to the development and maintenance of cross-sex friendship may be uncovered by identifying the reasons that close, cross-sex friendships terminate; therefore, I will provide excerpts from surveys and interviews with persons who have experienced the dissolution of such a friendship.

STRUCTURAL OPPORTUNITIES FOR THE DEVELOPMENT OF CROSS-SEX FRIENDSHIP

In the first study of cross-sex friendship, Booth and Hess (1974) emphasized the structural opportunities and normative constraints affecting the formation of the cross-sex friendships of middle-aged and elderly persons. Booth and Hess's findings suggest that education and social class mediate the experience of cross-sex friendship. Level of education played a role in the development of cross-sex friendship in that white-collar workers were more apt to have friends of the opposite sex than blue-collar workers were. Moreover, those friendship partners who were not similar to one another in age, social class, or education tended to parallel traditional man–woman relationships in that the men were older, more occupationally advantaged, and more educated than their female friends.

Booth and Hess (1974) also found that marital status and age exerted a significant influence on the formation of cross-sex friendships. Married persons reported less frequent interaction with cross-sex friends than with same-sex friends and a reduction in the amount of affect in cross-sex friendships. Age was also a factor in the formation of cross-sex friendships because, with increasing age, persons experienced a decline in the number of their cross-sex friendships. Gender appeared to interact with age since advancing age seemed to decrease the number of cross-sex friendships experienced by women compared to those experienced by men.

In fact, gender influenced the number of cross-sex friendships across the lifespan since men tended to form more cross-sex friendships than women did in this study. Booth and Hess (1974) believed that this finding was a result of men's experiencing a greater number of structural opportunities for interaction with the opposite sex out-side of marriage, as in the workplace, than women did.

More recent studies of cross-sex friendship have not focused on the structural opportunities for the development of cross-sex friend-ships. Yet embedded in these studies is comparable information about how age, sex, and marital status affect the formation of cross-sex friendships. The studies of Chown (1981) and Adams (1985) echo Booth and Hess's (1974) finding that with increasing age it is less likely that cross-sex friendships will develop and that in this regard age affects women more than men. Adams (1985) provides a normative explanation for elderly women's lack of male friends, arguing that elderly women define cross-sex friendship as a romantic relationship and that this definition reduces the potential number of men available for friendship. This definition appears to develop in part because elderly women lack models for nonromantic relationships with males of the same age. As middle-aged women, their cross-sex friendships were mediated by their husbands, wives of their male friends, or their jobs. In the social worlds of their adult years, nonmediated relation-ships with men were considered romantic in nature. Thus, as spouses and employment disappeared as mediating factors in elderly women's lives, their cross-sex friendships were considered romantic relation-ships. Adams's argument differs from and supplements Hess's (1972) early speculation that differential mortality rates for men and women set limits on the formation of cross-sex friendships for women, and this illustrates how structural factors and normative constraints merge to limit the opportunities for cross-sex friendships among elderly women.

As in Booth and Hess's (1974) study, other recent research finds that men consistently tend to report a higher occurrence of cross-sex friendships than women do. Wright (1989) averaged across noncollege samples of studies conducted by Bell (1981b), Block (1980), Booth and Hess (1974), and Rubin (1985) and stated that approximately 40% of the men and 30% of the women reported close cross-sex friend-ships. Rose (1985) also found a higher percentage of college men with cross-sex friends compared to college women with cross-sex friends.

The influence of marital status on the development of cross-sex friendship was also evident in the study conducted by Rose (1985). In her sample of 90 undergraduate and graduate students, 47% of the married women and 33% of the married men said they had no cross-sex friendships. In contrast, all of the single undergraduates and male graduate students and 73% of the single female graduate students in her sample reported their involvement in at least one cross-sex friendship. In addition to number, the results of this study also parallel Booth and Hess's (1974) findings that marital status influences the emotional closeness of cross-sex friendships. Married graduate students cited intimacy as a characteristic of their same-sex friendships rather than their cross-sex friendships more often than their unmarried counterparts did. Likewise, Block (1980) stated that only 6 out of 100 married persons named a cross-sex friend in his survey. And in Rubin's (1985) sample of married or cohabitating persons, 78% of the men and 84% of the women did not have a cross-sex friend. Rubin found that those individuals who did have a cross-sex friend after marriage tended to be professionals who married in their late 20s and thus came to the marriage with an established set of friends.

Only Weiss and Lowenthal (1975) reported a higher occurrence of cross-sex friendships among married persons in contrast to the studies of Rose (1985), Block (1980), and Rubin (1985). Sixty-six percent of the newlyweds in Weiss and Lowenthal's sample named a person of the opposite sex as one of their top three friends. These results must be qualified, however, because the participants were newlyweds and might therefore still have their premarital friendship sets intact.

Finally, persons' conceptions about the possibility of developing a cross-sex friendship is also influenced by the potential friends' marital status. In Lampe's (1985) study, 90% of his sample of college students believed that both husbands and wives should be able to have a cross-sex friendship, yet only 70% of these students answered similarly when asked if they would encourage or allow *their* spouse to have a cross-sex friend. This contradiction between their impersonal ideals and personal actualities seems to result from uncertainty about what is socially acceptable behavior regarding the cross-sex friendship of a married person. Half of Lampe's sample expressed concern about the difficulties inherent in managing a marital relationship and a friendship with a member of the opposite sex.

In sum, the influence of age, gender, and marital status on the formation of cross-sex friendship is consistently documented in the literature. The major findings are as follows: (1) older persons are less likely than younger persons to have a cross-sex friend, (2) males are more likely than females to experience cross-sex friendship, and (3) unmarried persons are more apt than their married counterparts to have cross-sex friendships and to experience a higher level of intimacy in cross-sex friendships.

Existing studies offer limited information regarding barriers to the formation of cross-sex friendship because researchers have restricted their investigations to the variables of age, sex, marital status, and level of education. While these variables may influence the likelihood of developing a friendship between men and women, other factors, such as physical settings, personal predispositions, attitudes and values, mutual friendships, commitments to other relationships, work, social activities, and the normative environment, should also be taken into account. In other words, cross-sex friendship development must be understood as an involved, dynamic process. Ting-Toomey (1989) alludes to this dynamism when she states:

> Interpersonal relationship development is a complex, multi-faceted process. It evolves and changes because of many intrinsic and extrinsic factors within and beyond the relationship. The relationship itself can transform the lives of the individuals in the relationship, and the individuals themselves can also actively monitor the progress of the relationship. The relationship transforms or develops, progresses or regresses within the larger social and cultural matrices. (p. 371)

The following "friendship development" stories highlight the structure of opportunities for cross-sex friendship development and the complexity involved in the process. Obviously, the men and women whom I interviewed had the opportunity to meet, interact, and develop a friendship with one another. These bonds developed as the men and women worked together, attended school, and spent time with mutual friends or family members. These women and men stated that their friendship grew as they found that they shared mutual interests, enjoyed the same types of activities, had similar life experiences, or "just enjoyed talking with one another." In short, like most relationships, these cross-sex friendships developed out of everyday activities and interactions.

Next, I present extended descriptions of the development of two cross-sex friendship dyads. The first friendship story is in many ways prototypical in nature since, at the time of their meeting, both friends were in college, were single; they met through mutual friends. The second story is less typical because, at their friendship's onset, the friends were in their mid-30s and had career and family responsibilities. The second story notes several barriers to the development of cross-sex friendship and describes how they may be overcome.

PHYL AND RON

Phyl, 33 years old, and Ron, 36 years old, met through a mutual friend at college and have been close friends for 16 years. While at college, Ron and Phyl developed a circle of friends who are still close today. When I asked Ron how he and Phyl began their friendship, Ron stated:

> "She was friends with my roommate when I graduated from college. And so, she was part of a group. There were, like, 10 or 12 of us that hung out together back then, and we were notorious. We did terrible things, and she was just part of the group and we became good friends."

When I asked Ron why he thought he and Phyl "hit it off," he replied:

> "We had similar interests. We liked to party a lot. We hung out at the pool together. We'd go to bars and drink together. We were all singles at the time, the group of us. She wasn't dating, and I wasn't dating anybody seriously, so it was real easy for us to go out and do things together without somebody else getting upset about it. It started out as just casual friends."

I asked Ron when he started thinking of Phyl as a close friend, he said: "When we'd sit around and get drunk and start talking about deep things. It was a gradual development."

Phyl related the story of their friendship in the following way:

"I met him through Mike. They had an apartment together. Mike I knew through school. There was a group of us of about 8 or 10, I guess, and we just always just kind of did stuff together. The group kind of came most through college, and then people came in that way. Then Sandy and I had an apartment together, and we had a pool, and it got to be this—our door was literally open. and everybody just came over to our pool all day Saturday and Sunday, and then we just did other things. This circle was being set up of, okay, this is what we do, Saturday and Sundays, and this is the group that does it."

I asked Phyl when she realized that she and Ron were friends, she replied:

"I can't, it's hard. I don't think that's anything that's just like, oh, this is Fourth of July and, oh, we're very good friends. I think I started using him as like a date for things. I wasn't involved [in a dating relationship], so when something came up, I'd ask him. And if something came up and he wasn't involved with someone, he asked me. There was never any, I mean, it was always understood to be that . . . I mean, would you mind going with me? Obviously. And obviously, if I was dating someone, I wouldn't have asked him and vice versa. I think maybe that's maybe where it [the friendship] started coming."

The structure of Phyl and Ron's lives encouraged the development of their friendship. First, they met while in college, a time of life often called "the golden friendship years" because the opportunities for friendship are very high. Second, both were single at the time of their meeting, and their activities, at least at first, took place in the context of a group of mutual friends. As Ron noted, it was "easy" for

Phyl and him to do things together because neither had commitments to romantic relationships. Conversely, if they had such commitments, they may have experienced more difficulty in developing their friendship. At the time of the development of their friendship, neither Ron nor Phyl experienced questions about their friendship from others in their friendship group. The group consisted of men and women, and everyone "assumed" that they were all "just friends" (although newcomers to the group and the families of Ron and Phyl asked them about the nature of their relationship). Their friendship developed, then, in a supportive normative climate.

The importance of these factors from their early friendship was underscored at the time I interviewed Ron and Phyl. By then, Phyl had gotten married and Ron was engaged to be married. Both friends were very busy with their careers. The structure of their lives had changed considerably since their first meeting, and both friends expressed regret that they were not able to spend more time together, stating that they usually included their partners in their activities because of a lack of time for socializing. Because of their long history together, Phyl and Ron were able to weather periods of separation and the various changes that took place in their relationship. However, Ron stated that if they had met during this later time of their lives, developing a friendship would have been difficult, if not impossible, because of their commitments to their romantic partners and their careers.

JOY AND RUSS

Joy, 37 years old, and Russ, 34 years old, have been close friends for 3 years. Joy is married and the mother of three children. Russ is single and not involved in a serious romantic relationship. Russ's and Joy's brothers were best friends in high school, so they had known each other for a long period of time. Even so, it was not until Russ and Joy started working together as choir directors for a church that they developed a close friendship. Joy and Russ cited their love of music as central to the development of their friendship. Joy described their friendship development in the following way:

"We were . . . we were working as music staff for the church. I was children's choir director. He was adult choir director. So . . . so some situations made us be together. Um, I think another reason was we had similar . . . we both had had fathers who died very young, and I think that gave us some initial contact in terms of understanding. And we both have challenging brothers to deal with. But, you know, we can immediately connect on those issues. I think probably the biggest reason, um, would have to be the music though."

When I asked Joy how she and Russ realized that they were friends, she replied:

"I . . . I remember one incident in particular that . . . that I realized there was somebody who understood. And it would have been after choir one night, and we stayed out in the parking lot and talked for, I don't know, a long time about the death of his father and how he was dealing with it and how his siblings were dealing with it . . . that whole experience. And I was further down that road than he was. So I could say, 'Oh, yeah. That's normal or . . . ' You know.

"And I understood that somebody else was seeing the same . . . you know, that I was not abnormal in the feelings I was having and the frustrations I was having as well. We both were children who were left here in town, and our moms were here, and all of his brothers and sisters were all gone, and my brother was gone. So, we were the ones left with our mothers, left with dealing with all of it daily, you know. And in those terms I remember thinking at that point, 'You know, this was somebody. Gee, he understands.' And that was nice."

Russ's story is similar to Joy's as he recounted the beginning of their friendship:

"Well, I was best friends with her brother. I never saw Joy very much. I spent time around their house, but she was never there. She was off with Jerry [her boyfriend] somewhere.

"Then we started working together at the church. I was director of the choir, and we started staff meetings, and, I don't know, we just started hanging out together, and we had a very common experience. Her dad was sick and died, and mine was sick and died. I don't know, we just have . . . we both have a love for music, and it's just one of those things. There was just that energy there. Auto, you know, right off the bat."

Given the influence of age and marital status on the development of cross-sex friendship reviewed above, Joy and Russ beat the odds when developing their friendship. Even so, Joy and Russ were very much aware of how Joy had to "juggle" her family life in order to devote time to the friendship. They planned their activities with one another during the day when Joy's children were at school or around their participation in such musical events as plays and recitals. Both stated that they worked hard to maintain a positive relationship with Joy's husband. Further, Joy and Russ experienced much public scrutiny of their friendship since they lived in a small town. Joy estimated that half the people in their small town believed that she and Russ were having an affair. Thus, the scrutiny led to the spread of rumors that the two were having an affair and led to direct questions from friends and family about the nature of their relationship. Plainly, Joy and Russ were able to develop and continue their friendship in contexts that were not entirely supportive of the development. However, both friends said that the friendship was worth the effort that it took to navigate in a less than favorable normative environment.

The above stories emphasize the involved nature of forging a cross-sex friendship since the process must reconcile personal predispositions, social networks, and norms involving acceptable woman–man relationships and behavior. In many instances such reconciliation is not achieved. The persons whom I interviewed who successfully negotiated a close cross-sex friendship believed that the process required a sustained effort and commitment by both friends. My participants believed that the friendship was valuable enough to warrant this commitment. However, other persons may perceive the effort as too costly or futile and may avoid developing and sustaining such a relationship.

This claim is supported by the results of a recent survey of men and women who, at the time of the survey, did not have a close friendship with a member of the opposite sex (Werking, 1994a). The participants in this study reported a variety of impediments to the development and maintenance of a close cross-sex friendship. The most frequently mentioned reason was involvement in either a dating or marital relationship (one-third of the cited reasons). This observation indicates that the establishment and maintenance of romantic relationships structure the participants' involvement in other opposite-sex relationships.

For many people, cross-sex friendships threaten the existence of their romantic relationships and therefore is avoided. This threat is explicitly addressed through partners' insecurity or jealousy or is acknowledged by reference to the "inappropriateness" of an intimate relationship with an opposite-sex person other than a romantic partner. This uneasiness is reflected in the following responses:

> "My present boyfriend gets jealous when I'm with guy friends, and it's not worth fighting all the time. *(Woman, 21 years old)*

> "I'm currently in a romantic relationship and experience friction in that relationship because of opposite-sex friends. My partner doesn't understand the need to seek intimate relations outside of romantic relations." *(Man, 22 years old)*

> "As a married woman, it seems to be inappropriate for me to have a male friend that I confide in, aside from my husband." *(Woman, 25 years old)*

The lack of opportunity to initiate a cross-sex friendship was mentioned frequently by the participants. The development of cross-sex friendship takes time, proximity, and initiative. Many of the participants either had a limited amount of time to invest in friendship or did not meet potential friends in their workplace or through their social networks. This finding echoes O'Meara's (1994) contention that the social and work lives of women and men continue to be segregated and thus prohibit the formation of cross-sex friendships. The following descriptions typify the participants' responses:

"My daily routine isolates me from most relationships. I also work in a predominately masculine profession." *(Man, 20 years old)*

"Because of my major—few males in my classes. So busy with work—again few males." *(Woman, 20 years old)*

Another frequently mentioned response was the potential for sex and romance in the cross-sex friendship dyad. This result reflects the current cultural debate about whether or not men and women can engage in nonsexual, intimate relationships with one another. Many of the participants in this survey apparently believed that men and women cannot be friends with one another without becoming romantic or sexual with one another since they cite this reason for not engaging in a cross-sex friendship.

This belief may be a result of past experiences with cross-sex friendships. Eighty percent of the sample said that they once had a close cross-sex friend. And nearly one-quarter of this group reported that their past friendships had ended because one or both of the friends desired a romantic relationship and that desire had either been rejected or the romantic relationship had not been successful. It appears, then, that this past experience has shaped many of the participants' willingness to participate in future cross-sex friendships.

Lastly, several of the survey respondents (14%) expressed a preference for same-sex friendship. Of this group, several people stated that they relate better to same-sex friends. This category of reasons contained the sharpest criticism of the opposite sex, with both men and women condemning the other sex's behavior in relationships. Overall, however, such criticism constituted only a small portion of the sample's responses.

The above interview and survey data highlight several issues affecting the development of cross-sex friendships, such as romantic relational status, attitudes toward the possibilities for platonic woman–man bonds, norms of the larger social environment, preferences for same-sex interaction, and commitments to career and family. These issues are ongoing concerns throughout the life of a cross-sex friendship. Many men and women are successful in addressing these concerns since they have developed enduring cross-sex friendship bonds; however, other friendship dyads are unable to manage these issues, and friendships dissolve. In addition to studying men and women who avoid cross-sex friendships, examining the dissolution of cross-sex friendships provides interesting insights into the problematic issues facing men and women as they negotiate platonic relationships with one another. I now consider the reasons that cross-sex friendships end.

THE DISSOLUTION OF CLOSE CROSS-SEX FRIENDSHIPS

The dissolution of friendship in general has rarely received the attention of scholars (Duck, 1982) since the bulk of the research attention has been directed toward the processes by which marital or dating relationships have terminated (e.g., Baxter, 1985; Duck, 1982; Orbuch, 1992; Vaughan, 1986). Although a handful of same-sex friendship dissolution studies exist, only one study (Werking, 1994a) has examined how or why cross-sex friendships end. A description of the study's sample and data collection techniques appears in the appendices.

As noted in Table 3.1, the most frequently mentioned termination reason was that the cross-sex friends grew apart from one another. Under this general category, physical separation was by far the most prevalent reason for friends' losing contact with one another. Physical separation was a result of attending different colleges, moving to other geographical locations, and changing jobs or class schedules.

The above termination reason is not unique to cross-sex friendship. However, the next two categories of reasons center around the issues of romance and sexuality, issues that tend to be particular to cross-sex friendship. Taken together, 48% of the described close friendships ended because a romantic relationship between the friends was not successful, one of the friends wanted a romantic relationship and that desire was not reciprocated, one or both of the friends became romantically involved with someone else, or third parties to the friendship assumed that the friendship was romantic in nature. The following quotations are samples of the responses in these categories:

"Because my feelings grew beyond friendship, and I believe he felt uncomfortable with the situation because he didn't feel the same way." *(Woman)*

"We both thought that since we were such good friends, that we would be great lovers. However, we were not, and our romantic interlude stopped as did our friendship." *(Man)*

"He met and began dating one particular woman [his wife eventually], thus it was no longer appropriate for us to hang around together. As a threesome, we could all get along. However, it is not the same after the two of us shared so many great times for so many years. At first we still ran around and called each other. But the more serious his relationship got with his girl-

TABLE 3.1. Categories of Reasons for Friendship Termination

Total number of reasons = 147

Category	Frequency	Percentage of total
I. *Friends who grew apart*	*50*	*35*
Physical separation	30	22
Divergence of values/goals	9	6
Social Distance	7	5
Lack of Time	4	2
II. *Romance/sexuality (within dyad)*	*36*	*24*
One friend's desire for romance	25	17
Mutual interest in romance, mutual backing away	11	7
III. *Romance/sexuality (third party)*	*36*	*24*
One or both friends becoming involved in a romantic relationship	20	13
Outsiders' assuming a romantic relationship	16	11
IV. *Violation of friendship expectations*	*21*	*14*
Dislike of friend's behaviors/ attitudes	19	13
Loss of trust	2	1
V. *Miscellaneous reasons*	*4*	*3*
Other	3	2
Uncertain	1	1

friend, there was no choice and to do the right thing and not threaten their growing relationship. So we ended ours." *(Woman)*

"It was hard to remain friends because of all the people— friends—that assumed we were 'more than friends.' It became so intense we tried to ignore comments. It ended because he be- came very involved in a girlfriend who did not even care to know my name, which was fine. But, she put pressure on him not to see, talk, look, etc. at me or else." *(Woman)*

Clearly, this study reveals that managing romance and sexuality both within the dyad and with members of the friends' social net- works poses obstacles for cross-sex friends and that these obstacles may lead to the demise of close friendships. In Chapter 4, I will focus exclusively on the issue of romance and sexuality within cross-sex friendships and will describe the manner in which men and women handle this issue.

In addition to investigating the primary reason for friendship dissolution, this study also explored the strategies that cross-sex friends use to dissolve their relationships. Thirty-eight percent of the sample said their friendships simply faded away. This process often took several months to complete and was not an intentional strategy since several respondents stated that they realized that the friendship was in trouble only after contact had ceased. Other people said that they abruptly cut off communication with their friends (23%) or intentionally avoided the friends by not frequent- ing usual meeting places, not socializing with mutual friends, or not returning phone calls (17%).

Only 15% of the sample said that they had explicitly talked about their friendships prior to ending them. One striking aspect of these data is the absence of repair strategies reported by the respondents (only 5% reported attempts to repair their friendships). These results indicate that cross-sex friends may avoid conflicts with one another, may find difficulties in the friendship too sensitive to discuss (such as romantic or sexual desires), and/or may regard their relationships as a taboo conversational topic.

CONCLUSION

Taken together, studies of cross-sex friendship development and dissolution reveal many impediments to close cross-sex friendships. It appears, in general, that close cross-sex friendships develop and continue *in spite of* rather than *because of* their social environments. Often, researchers have offered individualistic explanations for the lack of cross-sex friendships. The above discussion, however, lends credence to including the structural properties of persons' lives in such explanations. It appears that the configuration of persons' lives—their entanglements in work and personal relationships, the structure of work and school environments, their past experiences with platonic woman–man relationships, and the internalization of social or contextual norms regarding man–woman relationships—play a role in facilitating or restraining the development of enduring close cross-sex friendships.

The development of cross-sex friendship is indeed an involved process, and cross-sex friendship researchers have just begun to tap into this complexity. I urge researchers to take the study of cross-sex friendship development from the "netherlands of academic interest" (O'Meara, 1994, p. 4) and to design studies that will enhance understanding of the processes involved in forming and sustaining them.

Researchers should also broaden their focus from individual properties to features of the larger social context. Acknowledging the "landscape" (Lannamann, 1991) against which cross-sex friendship is enacted provides a richer picture of the *possibilities* for the development and sustenance of cross-sex friendship since these possibilities are shaped by forces larger than individual dyads. Finally, I believe that future research will benefit from the continued collection of detailed development stories from persons involved in established or dissolved cross-sex friendships. These stories provide insights into the intersection of larger social forces and dyadic practices, for, through these stories, persons articulate felt constraints and mutually negotiated behaviors within ever-changing social contexts.

4

The Private Side
of Cross-Sex Friendship III
Managing Romance and Sexuality

BONNIE AND BRAD

Bonnie, 22 years old, is white, heterosexual, single, and a college student. Brad, 24 years old, is white, heterosexual, unmarried, and a college graduate. They have been close friends for 7 years.

Brad

> Well, we really haven't . . . Well, we did address it [romance and sexuality] once, I guess, um, in Atlanta.

Bonnie

> Yeah.

Brad

> I don't know, it was kind of a spur of the moment thing.

Bonnie

> Yeah.

Brad

> It really didn't take a lot of thought or whatever behind it. It was just somethin' that happened. Uh, I mean it didn't carry out as far . . . *(Laughs)* as far as it could!

Bonnie

> *(Laughs)*

Brad

> But, you know, I don't know, it kinda helped me. I mean when all that happened, I didn't want to lose you as a friend. I mean— don't get me wrong—that night was wonderful and all, and I'm just . . . I'm glad there weren't any ill feelings, you know, towards what happened.

Bonnie

> Mm hmm, mm hmm.

Brad

> That would discontinue our friendship. And, um, . . .

Bonnie

> 'Cause we really haven't addressed . . . well, we joke around about things.

Brad

> I know we have. Yeah, we have, we joked about it, you know. Like if I call you or you call me and say, "What are you wearin'?" I mean, "What are you doin'?" Say, I just got out of the shower or whatever.

Bonnie

> *(Laughs)*

Brad

> And you're like, "Oh!" or whatever. And we've always joked about it. I don't know, the issue just came up.

Bonnie

> Came up. Sure did! *(Laughs)*

Brad

> What do you? . . . I mean, we've never really discussed this.

Bonnie

> We never really have.

Brad

No, we've never discussed it when that happened. We really didn't say anything. I mean, I was kind of not afraid, I mean, but I didn't know how you felt about it. And I wasn't going to ask you. Not that I was embarrassed or anything, but, um, I was just kind of concerned that our friendship might have been spoiled. So, now I'm asking you, what were you thinking?

Bonnie

(Laughs) That's what I was concerned about—if something did happen. I was scared. First, of all, I was scared about . . . we had such a great friendship. We still do. But if something *did* happen between us, would that ruin our friendship? I know that's something awful to think about whenever you get involved with somebody—if it's going to ruin something or not. But, um, before we just never addressed it. I think we kinda had, like, our boundaries, and we just knew what to do. I mean, we just kind of took it as we were friends. Because if we went any farther than that then . . .

Brad

It would have broke the boundaries.

Bonnie

Definitely. Then, that night in Atlanta, which I loved. That was a great night, and I don't know what I'm trying to say. *(Laughs)* Um, how did I feel about the issue? *(Laughs)* I mean that I felt that it was great. I was kind of confused. And it's not that I didn't want to say, "Brad, we ought to settle down." I was . . . I also had this other side of me saying, "I am still a friend of Linda's [his ex-girlfriend], and I'm being a bad friend." And I was just really confused. I was torn *(pause)* about what I should do and what I shouldn't do.

Brad

I was really confused too about the whole situation. About, I don't know, it's not that I hadn't thought . . .

Bonnie

It's not that I hadn't thought about it or hadn't considered it . . .

Brad

Right, right.

Bonnie

. . . Or I wouldn't have talked to my aunt about how I felt.

Brad

Right, I had thought about it. I don't know if I . . . I guess I had considered it also. But like you say, we were really close as friends and stuff. And I mean, if something came into it otherwise, that would be fine. But, uh, I don't know. Like you say, there was too many other things that were involved, such as Linda and such as . . . I don't know, it was a difficult situation that I feel went as far as it should at the time. You know if something arose later in time, then, um, I don't know.

Bonnie

It was kinda like . . . and also the next day it was like this had never *happened*! *(Laughs)*

Brad

I know, I know. *(Laughs)* It was like we didn't talk about it.

Bonnie

We didn't talk about it! And we never really have talked about it, have we?

Brad

No, we haven't.

Bonnie

We joke about it.

Brad

No, we never . . .

Bonnie

We just kind of left it where it was, and then that was it.

Brad

Yeah. *(Pause)* It was an odd situation. A situation, like I said, that I had thought about before—if I was ever in that situation what I would do. But, um, I don't guess you can ever know what's actually goin' to happen until it does happen, and then you have to make some decisions. Like I said, I think we were both kind of confused about what was actually going on.

Bonnie

I think so too.

Potential romance and sexually expressed affection between cross-sex friends fuels the debate over whether bonds between women and men can be "purely platonic." Consistently, in my conversations about cross-sex friendship with my students, audience members at scholarly conferences, friends, and colleagues, I am asked the question, "Is it possible for men and women to be close friends without engaging in sexual or romantic activity?" In asking this question, the questioner assumes that sexual activity constitutes the core of man–woman relationships (Rawlins, 1994) and thus that sexual and romantic feelings are part and parcel of woman–man relationships. This assumption is not surprising because of the privileging of a romantic heterosexual ideology in middle-class American culture, a point I have tried to make throughout this book. To be sure, sex and romance are important issues in the context of *some* cross-sex friendships; however, as I will describe in this chapter, these issues are not necessarily salient in all cross-sex friendships for a variety of reasons.

Unfortunately, cross-sex friendship researchers also adopt and perpetuate a heterocentric view of cross-sex friendship. First, we assume that the participants in studies are heterosexual men and women, or we specifically sample only heterosexual men and women (e.g., Rose, 1985; Sapadin, 1988) and thus neglect other forms of cross-sex friendship, specifically friendships involving gay men and lesbians. Second, we assume that romance and sexuality constitute ongoing concerns only in cross-sex friendships rather than acknowledge that these concerns may be raised in varying degrees in same-sex friendships between homosexual and/or heterosexual persons (Nardi, 1992; Rawlins, 1994). The bulk of my work as well has focused on friendship between heterosexual men and women, in large part because of my interest in the interplay between cultural assumptions (we live in a heterocentric culture) and friendship practices. This interest, however, does not excuse me from the criticisms that I level at other research, and it is my goal to expand my work to examine cross-sex friendship among homosexuals and between homosexuals and heterosexuals.

The review of the literature addressing the topic of romance and sexuality presented here clearly reflects a heterocentric orientation toward the investigation of this topic. However, as noted above, I wish to open up the discussion of romance and sexuality by including a homosexual perspective on cross-sex friendship. This chapter is thus divided into three sections.

The first section reviews studies that have investigated sexuality between heterosexual friends. These studies have used the term *sexuality* to describe overt sexual activity between male and female friends or the possibility that such activity might occur between the friends. I use this term in similar ways in my studies.

The second section describes how heterosexual men and women manage these issues in their friendships. This section presents the results of my interviews with 50 pairs of close cross-sex friends. It discusses the process through which close cross-sex friends negotiate relationships in which behaviors that might be given romantic or sexual meanings in other forms of man–woman relationships are not interpreted as such in the context of their friendships. I chose to include only data obtained from individual interviews with *both* partners of a cross-sex friendship because obtaining both persons' perspectives on the issues of romance and sexuality provides a richer portrait of how these issues are managed. I first address how men and women create stabilized relational definitions. Then I focus on friends who have experienced difficulty in managing romance and sexuality in their relationship because of uncertainty about the nature of their relationship. Thus, this section explores the ramifications of involvement in a close woman–man relationship whose definition is ambiguous or unstable in nature.

The third section of this chapter addresses the issues of romance and sexuality in friendships where one friend or both are homosexuals. The literature in this area is meager; therefore, my comments are meant to be generative rather than conclusive.

ROMANCE AND SEXUALITY IN THE CONTEXT OF FRIENDSHIP BETWEEN HETEROSEXUAL WOMEN AND MEN

Many authors (e.g., Bell, 1981a; O'Meara, 1989; Rawlins, 1982; Rubin, 1985) have commented on the potential problematics involved in managing the sexual dimension of a platonic woman–man friendship. Few studies (Bell, 1981a; Furman, 1986; Rubin, 1985; Sapadin, 1988), however, have actually gathered and analyzed data addressing this issue. According to the results of these studies, romance and sexuality are problematic issues for cross-sex friends. For example, in a survey of professional men and women conducted by Sapadin (1988), the participants most frequently answered "sexuality" in response to the question, "What do you dislike most about your cross-sex friendships?"

With that response in mind, it appears that persons may view sexuality in cross-sex friendships as a potentially negative feature. From this perspective, sexual involvement between friends is seen as a threat to friendship (Bell, 1981a; Sapadin, 1988) that inhibits the full-fledged development of cross-sex friendships (Bell, 1981b). Bell (1981a) found that "conventional" men and women were especially concerned about the sexual dangers inherent in cross-sex friendships and guarded against allowing physical attraction to affect their relationships. Moreover, conventional men reported engaging in few cross-sex friendships, and both conventional men and women reported lower levels of intimacy in their cross-sex friendships (Bell, 1981a).

The possibility that men and women may have sexual or romantic motives for initiating a cross-sex friendship may also inhibit the development of that type of friendship (Werking, 1994a). Males often acknowledge sexual attraction as a reason for developing cross-sex friendships (Rose, 1985). And women in this same study frequently stated that men's motives made them distrustful of male friendship overtures (Rose, 1985).

Predictably, other gender differences emerge in studies examining this issue. In addition to a higher tendency to view sexual attraction as a motive for developing cross-sex friendships, men also are more likely to believe that having a sexual relationship adds deeper feelings and closeness to their cross-sex friendships (Sapadin, 1988) and that sexual partners can become their friends (Sapadin, 1988). In addition to these differences in the responses of men and women regarding sexuality in cross-sex friendship, similarities in their responses should also be noted. Specifically, men and women tend to keep their friendships and sexual relationships separate, although sexual feelings and tension remain present in their friendships (Sapadin, 1988).

Obviously, the possibility of a sexual relationship developing between cross-sex friends does not prohibit all cross-sex friendships from occurring. As a possibility, however, it does continue to affect the ongoing management of cross-sex friendships. Rubin (1985) reports that most of the participants in her interviews insisted that engaging in sexual activity with a cross-sex friend paved a certain path to conflict.

An inability to decide mutually whether or not cross-sex friends will engage in sex frequently leads to the demise of cross-sex friendships or their redefinition as primarily a romantic involvement (Bell, 1981b; Rubin, 1985). Still, there also appears to be a positive perspective on the possibility of sex in cross-sex friendships. Many participants in studies discussed their enjoyment of the underlying sexual dimension in their cross-sex friendships (Bell, 1981b; Furman, 1986; Rubin, 1985; Sapadin, 1988). Both men and women believed that sexual attraction in cross-sex friendships validated their attractiveness. Others commented that sexual attraction added a "zest" to their relationships (Rubin, 1985). A few participants in Rubin's study differentiated between "friendly, almost platonic sex" and "romantic sex" (p. 150). For these individuals, sexuality was incorporated into the framework of their friendships and did not impinge upon their ability to be friends with one another.

It seems, then, that the question of whether or not cross-sex friends will incorporate a sexual dimension into their relationship is an ongoing issue in many friendships between heterosexual women and men. For some people, the possibility of sexuality deters them from engaging in cross-sex friendships; for others, it is a "totally appropriate natural feeling" (Furman, 1986, p. 118), which may or may not be expressed. Even so, the majority of participants in the reviewed studies did not act upon their sexual attraction for one another because of the potential threat to their friendship. However, a few participants have become sexual partners and, according to them, have successfully incorporated a sexual dimension into their friendships.

Upon reviewing the existing literature, it is apparent that by having gone no further than eliciting acknowledgment from cross-sex friends that it is an issue in their friendships, studies addressing sexuality in cross-sex friendship have just begun to touch on how friends manage this issue (Nardi & Sherrod, 1994). In the interviews I conducted with heterosexual cross-sex friends, therefore, I attempted to fill in gaps in our knowledge about this issue by questioning the friends extensively about the role of romance and sexuality in their relationships (Werking, 1992).

Before describing the results of the interviews, I elaborate on the points made in the introductory chapter to this book regarding the interdependence of societal and relational practices. The focus of the present chapter is on relational practices, addressing the role of context, interaction, and meaning construction in composing the nature of relationships. However, the connection between these concepts and the societal context is explored throughout the chapter.

Cross-Sex Friendship as a Context for Interaction

A relationship may be viewed as a context for action in that ongoing relationships develop their structure from the patterns of meanings that are "built up" and composed over time via the actions of the relational partners (Rawlins, 1987). Further, the relationship and the acts of the partners are intertwined since the relationship is constituted by the partners' actions and, in turn, shapes their practices. Thus, the relationship is of a higher logical type than the punctuated stream of practices constituting and constituted by the relationship. In essence, the relationship is a "meta-pattern" (Bateson, 1978) or a "context of contexts" (Bateson, 1991a, p. 208) for it provides the overarching context for the concrete practices of the relational partners (Rawlins, 1987). As such, concrete practices may be understood by their producers when viewed in the context of a relationship.

This point is particularly salient when investigating the negotiation of cross-sex friendship. This is so because, to an observer, many of the practices described by close cross-sex friends could be construed as being romantic or sexual in nature unless those practices are interpreted from the point of view of the participants, whose perspective is inherently contextualized by the meaning structures created in their everyday friendship interactions.

The societal context of cross-sex friendship "frames" these interactions. As discussed earlier, participants in cross-sex friendships must navigate a relationship within an ambiguous cultural context. In other words, mainstream culture provides few "context markers" (Bateson, 1972b) that classify or define a man–woman relationship as a friendship. Instead, a man and woman may have to rely on ambiguous or contradictory cues as they attempt to achieve mutual understanding of the nature of their relationship.

Thus, would-be cross-sex friends are compelled to obtain their information about the definition of the relationship primarily from the assortment of behaviors constituting their relationship (Bateson, 1972b). Bateson (1963) states:

> The problem, then, for every individual in every interchange is to maintain an up-to-the minute grasp of understanding of the state of contingency patterns between himself and his *vis-à-vis*. Consciously or unconsciously, he has to be able to recognize what sorts of triagrams, or more complex sequences, should characterize the relationship at every moment and to act in terms of these recognitions. The individual has to predict from what occurred previously which pattern is appropriate at the moment. This is what we call understanding between persons. (p. 181)

For a relationship to continue to be viable, each partner's understanding of the relational context must *correlate* with the understanding of the other (Berger & Kellner, 1964). In the instance of a cross-sex friendship, achieving a workable understanding may be especially challenging because of the minimal and conflicting guidelines provided by the cultural context in which it is enacted.

In order to understand my interviewees' perspectives on the issues of romance and sexuality in their friendships, I questioned them about how they handled romantic and sexual interest in their relationships. The questions specifically focused on whether the partners to a relationship had ever felt that they wanted the relationship to become romantic or sexual in nature—and, if so, how these feelings were handled. If a partner had not experienced romantic or sexual feelings for his or her friend, I asked the partner why this was so. In addition, I asked the friends questions about how they expressed affection for each other.

The Negotiation of Romance and Sexuality in Stabilized Cross-Sex Friendships

Given the limited positive cultural sanctions for close male–female platonic relationships, the participants' awareness of the nonnormative status of their friendships, and past research (i.e., Sapadin, 1988) reporting that managing sexuality in cross-sex friendship is one of its most problematic aspects, I was surprised to learn that 42 of the 50 participating pairs had never raised romance and sexuality as *serious* issues in their friendships. This is not to say that the friends had not *thought* about the issue, but they reported that there had never been serious or explicit consideration of becoming romantic and/or sexual with their partners.

Developing a Stabilized Relational Definition

The majority of the participating cross-sex friends described negotiating friendships in which sexuality or romance was not a major theme. This does not mean that nuances of sexuality and romance had never been present in these relationships, but that romance and sexuality were not significant issues. My confidence in this assessment of the type of friendship negotiated by these participants is enhanced because I interviewed both partners about the issues of romance and sexuality in their friendship. I also asked both partners about their perceptions of their friend's perspective on these issues.

As I analyzed friends' responses to my questions regarding sexuality, romance, and expressions of affection, I realized that my understanding of their descriptions was greatly enhanced by tracing the development of each of their relationships. In order to understand what these issues meant in *present* relationships, I had to consider what they had meant in the *past*.

These close cross-sex friendships involved high levels of emotional interdependence and commitment. In addition, typically the friends were verbally and nonverbally affectionate with one another: hugging, kissing, linking arms, and saying "I love you" to one another. In the present cultural milieu, such behaviors in an opposite-sex relationship have commonly come to represent expressions of romantic love to both the participants in the relationship and to outside observers. These behaviors took on different meanings, however, in the contexts of these friendships. Sue identified this difference in meaning in response to my question, "Do you think there is a relationship between your close cross-sex friendship and romance?"

> "Well, okay. First, to have a boyfriend you have to like the person before you can fall in love, and I think that you have to be friends—good friends—before any of that can happen. And so right there you get definite similarities—almost parallel. Then, that is where it starts getting different. Because holding hands isn't just a way to show that you are 'glad you're here. I'm so glad you made it. You drove carefully. I really missed you.' It's more of a 'I really like being with you. I want to get more serious.' And all of the similarities usually, . . . not *end*—because your boyfriend is still your friend—but it gets more complicated. Things take on new meaning."

Debbie also described the difference in meaning attached to behaviors when enacted in her friendship with Alex as opposed to her dating relationship with Tim:

"We [Alex and Debbie] can touch each other and nothing will happen. It doesn't mean a darn thing. We hold hands and hug each other. You know. But with Tim and I, we can do things like that, and it means something different."

Partners also talked about what the word *love* meant in the context of their friendship. It is interesting to note that they had some difficulty expressing this in large part, I believe, because we are not linguistically equipped to describe platonic male–female love. A woman said:

"One of the last things we say to each other every night is 'I love you.' Um, I've always known that I loved him, but, you know, just in that weird different sense, you know. To tell you the truth, I can't remember who said it first. Because, I mean, we both, we do, we love each other very much."

Her friend agreed, saying: "My feelings are more of love in a whole 'nother sense. And, you know, she's more family than she is anything else." Another woman described how she and her friend express their love for one another:

"I'll tell him . . . we have a thing, you know. It's like, 'I love you, Chris.' And he'll be like, 'Shut up, Linda.' We always, you know: 'I love you, Linda.' 'Shut up, Chris.' We just tell each other to shut up, so it's kind of like a very evasive kind of fun loving, you know. It's like, you tell each other you mean a lot to each other. If anything ever happened to Chris, it would kill me because I love him to death. He's my buddy."

Last, a woman talked about the use of the word *love* in her close cross-sex friendship: "You know, some people are kind of hesitant to use the word *love* in terms of their friends. But I think it definitely fits. *(Pause)* Because there are all different kinds of love."

The majority of the partners whom I interviewed seemingly had developed a relationship in which they could distinguish between behaviors with romantic and sexual undertones and those without such meanings. The question thus becomes: How did these partners negotiate a relational definition that enabled them to understand the meaning of potentially ambiguous behaviors? Answering this question necessitates charting how the cross-sex friendship developed and identifying patterns of meaning that coursed through the relationship, while remaining sensitive to the fluid, protean nature of these patterns as they responded to external and internal tensions. Thus, studying the development of relational definitions in a cross-sex friendship must take into consideration the personal predispositions, attitudes, and values of the participants as well as the social and cultural contexts within which the relationships developed.

Delia (1980) has suggested that the social context within which relational partners meet impinges on the relationship because the content proposes and constrains possible developmental pathways. Accordingly, I turn my focus to the circumstances surrounding the initial meetings and continued interaction of these cross-sex friends. These bonds developed as the friends worked together, attended school, and spent time with mutual friends or family members. As they interacted, they found that they shared mutual interests, enjoyed the same types of activities, had similar life experiences, or "just enjoyed talking with one another." In short, like most friendships, these dyads developed out of everyday activities and interactions.

The connection between the personal characteristics of partners, the definition of their cross-sex relationship, and their involvement in other relationships was readily apparent when I questioned them about why their relationship developed into one that they defined as friendship rather than romance. Their responses may be summed up in the following way. *Involvement in an intimate relationship with a person of the opposite sex can, at times, exhibit shades of romance; however, because of external and internal exigencies, romance and sexuality are downplayed. And over time, attributing romantic or sexual meaning to their own or their friend's behavior becomes less plausible.*

Various personal and social exigencies constrained the practices of these cross-sex relationships from their inception and continued to shape them at the time of our interviews. Commitments to other romantic and marital relationships, as well as sexual preference, seem to be the constraints that most affected these relationships at their start. Other concerns, such as incompatible behaviors (e.g., poor management of money or lack of ambition professionally) and attitudes and an unwillingness to sacrifice the friendship for a romantic relationship, grew out of the partners' interactions.

Internal and External Constraints on Cross-Sex Friendship Development

Friends' commitments to other romantic relationships impinged on these dyads during their infancy and continued to influence their definitions. Although participating in a romantic or marital relationship may not preclude other romantic relationships for everyone, it did for these participants. My married interviewees cited their marital status as a major factor in developing a "friendship" rather than a "romance." Hal discussed how his marriage helped define his cross-sex friendship by stating: "I was married when we became friends, so it was never possible for us to be anything else. It [romance] never came up between us."

Involvement in a dating relationship also shaped the way in which partners developed their cross-sex friendship since the dating relationship served as a "barrier" to romance in the developing friendship. This constraint is evident in one man's description of his first interaction with his female friend. I asked him, "How was your relationship initially defined? Did you think of her as a friend?" To which he responded:

> "Well, I was hitting on her! I asked her out, and she said, 'No, I have a boyfriend.' And I was like, 'Yeah, you're right. I have a girlfriend too.' *(Laughs)* In another city, you know. But then, uh, second semester, she moved into the same dorm I lived in, and we used to eat lunch and dinner together all the time . . . and just hung out.

Then I asked him, "So, you gradually started thinking of her as a friend rather than as somebody you were interested in dating?" To which he replied: "Well, after that she got engaged, and so I had no chance. And so we were buddies after that."

Here is part of a conversation between Joe and Mary in which they discussed how Joe's involvement in a dating relationship influenced their friendship:

Mary

> We resumed our friendship. We started working together and we started going . . .

Joe

> But I had a girlfriend. I had a girlfriend I've been datin' for, like, 5 years.

Mary

> Right. But we started hanging out, and the friendship flourished.

Joe

> There was never any question in your mind about . . . I couldn't be romantically involved with you because I had a girlfriend. So, that was one . . .

Mary

> I was just ecstatic to see you.

Joe

> Well, that's something you just have to get over! *(Laughs)* But, that was a nice barrier for us—to have . . . to have a cross-sex friendship.

Outside romantic interests helped define the relational parameters according to which these participants interacted. However, those parameters were further defined, and perhaps modified, during the course of interaction in response to other external constraints. In addition to outside romantic involvements, external influences included the partners' other third-party relationships, such as family or other friends, as well as changing geographical locations or employment. These dyads accommodated themselves to these external influences, which took time away from the friendship and also changed the friends' expectations about self and partner.

Involvement in an outside romantic relationship seemed to be a major impetus to developing a relationship defined as a "friendship" rather than a "romance" for my participants. Even so, similarities in life experiences, mutual interests in activities, enjoyable conversations, and the provision of emotional support were a few of the relational factors that partners cited as propelling their friendship from one that was casual in nature to one that was close.

Internal influences also helped define these cross-sex relationships as friendships from their initiation. One influence mentioned by friends included their personal preferences in romantic or sexual partners. Many of the friends stated that they simply never had a romantic or sexual interest in their partners. While they found their partners physically attractive, they were not attracted to them sexually.

An array of other types of internal influences also steered the relationship away from becoming romantic or sexual in nature. Through their interactions, friends became aware that their partners exhibited personal characteristics that they would find problematic in the context of a romantic relationship. These friends drew clear distinctions between romantic relationships and cross-sex friendships, recognizing differences in the relational goals, expectations, and norms for behavior suggested by each relational context. In the context of a friendship, behaviors, such as an inability to manage money or a lack of professional ambition, could be overlooked. But, in the context of a romantic relationship, they could not. Chris had, at one point in his friendship with Linda, wanted to become romantically involved with her. His interest was not reciprocated; and as we talked about that issue, he expressed relief that the romantic relationship had not evolved. In response to my question, "Have you ever felt romantic feelings creeping up again in your friendship?" he stated:

"I haven't felt those creeping up because I pretty much came to the conclusion that if we were to go out it wouldn't be too good because we're . . . in a way, we're kind of alike, you know. I guess also after a while we started seeing the other person's secrecies, I guess, and you start going 'Whew.' "

In response to the same question, Ron stated:

"I think there develops in the relationship where you go through a phase. Start out as a cross-sex relationship, and for one or the other it's very . . . one person or the other starts to look around and says, 'You know, I'm looking for someone to get serious about, but I'm having so much fun with this person, maybe this is the one.' And so you kind of go through an evaluation process. And then something happens to say, 'No, this isn't the one,' and you go back to just a cross-sex friendship situation."

When I asked Ron why he thought that he and his cross-sex companion had remained friends, he responded: "Because of our common interests. Sharing our history, we've been through so much together that has been fun that you don't want to let go." And when I asked Ron why he wanted to keep his cross-sex relationship at a friendship level, he replied:

"Our interests were not sufficient enough to sustain a close relationship. Some of her behaviors are just things that I said, 'If I had to live with this woman, I couldn't handle it.' As friends, we're fine."

The manner in which the friends enacted their romantic relationships also prevented the friendships from turning romantic in nature. For example, during a taped conversation after their individual interviews, Lynn and David, friends for 7 years, reflected on the reasons that they had never approached each other in a romantic or sexual way. Although they had difficulty pinpointing the reasons, through their conversation they eventually determined that it was their differing styles of "being in love." For example, they determined that Lynn liked to control her romantic partners, a characteristic that David found unappealing. In contrast, David liked to engage in many friendships while being in a romantic relationship, a preference, Lynn said, she "would find threatening because it takes too much attention away from me." Through the many years of their friendship, they had witnessed each other's romantic relationships and, thus, could easily identify each other's romantic style and assess the compatability of these styles.

In addition to finding a friend's behaviors problematic, the openness of a friendship also may prevent it from becoming romantic in nature. In other words, friends may know too much about one another to become romantic partners. Regarding this issue, one woman said:

"Sometimes, I think, you can know too much about a person . . . you know, you cross the line, more cliches here or whatever. But, I mean it's like part of, I think, a relationship—that type of relationship [romantic]—is the mystique, the mystery."

Angie and Steve discussed this aspect of their friendship in their conversation:

Angie

See, you know, there's not even . . . no offense, but I'm not attracted to you at all. Probably because I've known you for too long.

Steve

Yeah, and I scratch my butt.

Angie

And you scratch your butt. And you pick your toenails.

Steve

See, I think when you're with someone who you want to impress—maybe someone you lust after or whatever—and you want to lure them into bed, there's a certain amount of work you do to maintain an image that you want them to have of you— that . . . that you dress a certain way or you want to look a certain way in front of them all the time. You want . . . like the advertisers will dress up a hamburger to look really good in the advertisement. They put glue for mayonnaise on the bun, you know. People who want to impress each other and get each other into bed, I think, are going to put glue on their buns, right?

Angie

We're not.

Steve

> But we're not trying to impress each other, so we're being, you know, we'll be ourselves. We'll be totally open and revealing to each other, you know.

Finally, the friends cited their unwillingness to sacrifice the friendship as an important reason for them not to become romantically or sexually involved with one another. Romantic relationships, from the perspective of these participants, are unstable relationships. Because these men and women valued their friendships and wanted to ensure that their friends remained in their lives, they were reluctant to transform their friendships into romantic relationships. Over and over again, they told me that they had "worked too hard" for a friendship to sacrifice it for a potential romance. One man said: "I really like her friendship. And if we became boyfriend–girlfriend, that might be fine. But then we might lose a friendship."

A second man echoed this concern: "I'd rather not lose a good friend, you know, because you can always get another girlfriend. You can't replace a friend."

Similarly, in response to my question, "Why do you think you and your cross-sex friend have not become involved romantically?" one woman stated:

> "I enjoyed the friendship, and I still enjoy the friendship so much that . . . that creates tension that I see between males and females. . . . . [We were] starting to get a romantic relationship going, that I never wanted. I mean, I think, it takes longer for males and females that are romantically involved to get a friendship established longer than, um, ones that they are not. Because there's not that conflict."

An unwillingness to sacrifice the friendship, on the one hand, and incompatible behaviors and attitudes, on the other, were products of the friends' ongoing interactions that continued to shape the nature of their relationships. For, although a few of these friends described "phases" in which they considered becoming romantically intimate with their partners, they chose not to because of a complex of external and internal constraints.

Explicit Metarelational Talk as a Negotiation Strategy

These "phases" sometimes require explicit talk about the relationship, particularly when one partner desires to become romantically involved and the desire is not reciprocated. Such talk may be difficult for partners since the relationship may be at risk. Many of my participants reported avoiding talking about their feelings at times because they feared losing the relationship. Others engaged in such talk, although it was considered stressful because of the perceived risk of losing the friendship.

For example, Linda and Chris had wrestled with the issue of romance when Chris confessed to Linda that he was in love with her. This occurred soon after Linda left to attend a college located in a different city. Linda said that she was completely taken off guard by Chris's interest and didn't know quite how to respond. One way that Linda chose to handle the uncertainty was to avoid contacting Chris for several months. When she returned home for the Christmas holidays 3 months later, Linda said that she and Chris talked about their relationship "quite a bit." According to Linda,

> "I told him, you know, 'Chris, I love you to death but I've never felt that way about you, but that does not in any sense or form lower you in my eyes.' I mean I still hold him in the highest esteem."

Chris recalls this period in their relationship in the following way:

> "Probably the big one was when I got romantic feelings for her, and I tried to ignore it for a while because I couldn't make heads or tails what it was, you know. There's a huge gray area which nobody . . . which a lot of songs, poems, and movies, and everything is murky about. Is it friend or . . . you know? Basically the

When Harry Met Sally thing, you know, one of my favorite movies. Um, I didn't know how to handle it, you know. I never have been very successful in the romantic field. So finally I just decided, 'Well, we'll take that leap of fate, just like everybody else, and see what happens.'

"And, uh, I don't know what was going through her mind, but she just sort of took it in one ear and out the other, I guess. I don't know. We don't really talk about it that much. And then I said it again, and I think it finally stuck that time, and I don't think she really . . . it just out of left field to her. She just never saw it.

"So that kind of made a little tension for a while. Um, and then she was gone. She was going to college, she was ready to go to college, and, uh, she went in the fall. And I wrote her a letter, trying to make sure that she knew what I was, you know, and to make sure it was all clear. And she wrote me back, saying that she was flattered and that she never thought of me that way and stuff. And that kind of hurt, you know.

"And, so, she came back for Christmas. And ended up she was hanging around other people that I was hanging around with. And we met her at a party, and it was kind of hard, you know. And I was trying to go through it, 'Okay, we're friends. Accept this.'

"So I, like . . . I bought her a Steely Dan album that she didn't have, and she rejected it. She said no. And that kind of hurt too, but I kind of understood what she was talkin' about. 'Cause she said she didn't know how to handle it at the moment. I guess it was about from then on it took about a year and a half, two years before I next heard from her. I thought I totally blew the whole relationship, you know.

"I don't really think it was planned, like, 'Okay, I'm gonna talk to Chris again,' 'cause she called me. And that time I had started a new relationship. It just happened because she had just gone through a real bad thing with her boyfriend. A real bad incident. And she called me up, and she just said, 'Hey, let's get a band together.' And I was just, like, 'Wow. I haven't heard from you, and all of a sudden you're talkin' to me like time hasn't passed.' And I was like, 'I don't even know what my feelings are for you.'

"The band just established us back in the friendship again. When I . . . when I figured out, you know, that there weren't feelings and I was really in love with my girlfriend, and I was, like, okay."

For this cross-sex friendship pair, talking about their relationship helped to reduce the ambiguity about how the partners were perceiving the relationship. This talk allowed them to air their feelings, but did not reduce the tension between them. This tension resulted in a lengthy separation after which they were able to redefine their relationship as a friendship. Further, the rekindling of the friendship was facilitated by Chris's involvement in romantic relationship.

For other partners, talking about their relationship facilitated dismissal of the tension associated with one partner's romantic feelings toward the other. One man recalls that he had "gotten the feeling" that his friend was interested in becoming romantically involved with him. He said:

"I knew something was different. I hadn't seen her in a while, and she came home, and something had changed. We went out, and when I talked to other friends, she'd kind of get a little pushy, you know. And I'm, like, 'Whoa, whoa.' So, towards the end of the evening we were driving home, and I pulled off to the side of the road and basically set her straight on how things were going to be. And it was the hardest thing that I'd ever said to her. And we wept. And it was kinda a turning point in the relationship."

His friend also recalled that time as a turning point in their relationship. She seemed glad to know exactly where she stood with him and that he had been honest with her about his feelings. Since then, both partners believed that their friendship had grown closer.

To summarize, it is clear that the overwhelming majority of my interviewees had created a relational context that they mutually defined as a friendship. Further, they viewed friendship as a "connection of the mind" and a "spiritual bonding" rather than a relationship in which physical contact or expressions of affection assumed romantic or sexual meanings. The relational contexts were originally created, and continued to be created, via the exchange of implicit and explicit messages about the nature of the relationship. These messages emanated from the cultural and social environment in which the friendships were developed and from the partners as they responded to their environment and to one another.

For these friends, the relational definition had stabilized so that none of the friends viewed a shift toward a romantic definition as probable. My use of the word *stabilized* does not, however, imply that these relationships were static. On the contrary, they were in continuous motion as ever-changing configurations of internal and external concerns were managed (Rawlins, 1992). This variation, however, took place within the context of friendship or, as Bateson (1991d) states, "within the terms of the given system" (p. 61).

Internal and external concerns are managed much differently, however, when the relational partners do not mutually understand the nature of their relationship. In discussing this situation, I will highlight the friendships of Teresa and Tony and of Melissa and Bryan. Each of these friendships embodies one of two distinct themes evident in the eight friendships in which the friends wrestled with the meaning of romance and sexuality. As will be seen in these two friendships, interpreting the partners' behaviors was problematic because the friends were unable to identify with certainty the relational context within which their interactions took place.

The Negotiation of Romance and Sexuality in Unstable Cross-Sex Friendships

Teresa and Tony as well as Melissa and Bryan were engaged in relationships that they defined as friendships, but that definition was, at times, unstable as they attempted to reconcile their romantic feelings toward their partners. Teresa and Tony dated for 2 years prior to redefining their relationship as a close friendship. Melissa and Bryan had, as Bryan described it, "brushed the edges" of a romantic relationship several times. These two pairs of friends handled the uncertainty in their relationship in different ways. Both pairs seemed committed to making their friendships work but admitted that they felt frustrated and uncomfortable at times.

Teresa and Tony

Teresa and Tony referred to each other as "best friends." Teresa described how her friendship grew out of a dating relationship:

> "Well, basically, we became best friends at the same time we were dating. 'Cause he . . . like we were still dating, but he was also my best friend. Over time, we got to be better and better friends and, like, just everything we did. Like if I had something that I would go to a friend with, it was Tony that I'd go to. And then, um, the dating side started to not work out as well. We started not . . . we started having fights about things like I'd have with someone I was dating. So we just kind of ended that. But the friendship neither of us wanted to lose. So now we are best friends."

Tony stated: "We just thought, you know, we were good friends, and we thought it would be better as a friendship."

For Teresa and Tony, the redefinition of their relationship was mutual and gradual. They both stated that they were comfortable with the way in which their friendship was going but identified one recurring problem area in their bond: managing their romantic involvement with others. Teresa had been dating a man for several months. Her current romantic involvement and Tony's potential future involvement with a woman were topics that they found difficult to discuss with one another. I asked Teresa to discuss what she liked least about her friendship with Tony and she responded:

> "Trying to date other people and still be best friends with him. 'Cause since we used to date, I think it would hurt him. If we had just always been friends, it wouldn't at all. But since we used to date, some of it still hurts."

When I asked Teresa how she thought she would feel if Tony started dating someone else, she replied:

"Hurt, real hurt, but I'd have to get over it 'cause he's workin' real hard at not being mad at me. And so I'd be hurt and probably be real sarcastic and mean to him, but then slowly I'd get over it. And he knows, like, he knows when I am mad how to just deal with it. So he'd know what to do."

Teresa and Tony adopted the strategy of talking about their relational problems and about the nature of their relationship with one another. They monitored their relationship very closely, sometimes talking daily about problems and how to resolve them. They both believed that talking was the only way to make the relationship work. Tony said: "We just talk it out, just realize that this is what happened. Now we're friends, so this is what we are going to be. It's just a repositioning of how we feel."

Teresa said:

"Um, we just gotta talk through it, we just gotta be open. Being open is the most important, and we both kind of hold back some things on that, so we've got to work on that. So we keep talking about what is wrong, trying to work it out with each other instead of ignoring it."

Teresa and Tony both acknowledged that what they were trying to do was a difficult enterprise, although Teresa said, "If you care enough, it can work." The process was made more difficult by the responses of outsiders to their relationship. Tony said that many people did not believe him when he told them he and Teresa were friends. Tony lived in a fraternity during his college years and found the other males in the fraternity house were continually asking him about his relationship with Teresa. Teresa said that Tony "works too hard" at trying to demonstrate to his fraternity brothers that he and Teresa really were "just friends." Teresa stated that she also received questions from her friends and family about the nature of her relationship with Tony. When I asked her why she thought outsiders were curious, she said: "Since we used to date, nobody understands how we're still best friends. They think that when you break up with somebody, you're not going to be friends with them. So they wonder a lot about that." Teresa and Tony tried to ignore what other people said about their relationship, but nevertheless they found it annoying and had experienced several disagreements about how to handle outsiders' perceptions.

This friendship is an interesting example of how a redefinition of the relational context carries with it the premises for redefining the meaning of behaviors enacted within the context. Teresa and Tony still expressed their affection for one another by hugging and continued to say "I love you" to one another. Teresa said that touching one another came naturally because they used to date. The meaning of those behaviors had changed, however, since they had relabeled their relationship. As Tony stated earlier, "It's just a repositioning of how we feel." The difference in meaning of their demonstrations of affection was also evident in Teresa's description of her love for Tony:

"Just that you can really feel a love for . . . like a love for a friend that is different than dating. I just love him more than anything, so I guess that's it. Just that you can really love someone even if it's not like a romantic love at all. Just love."

By talking with one another, Teresa and Tony hoped to achieve a long-lasting friendship. Both of them were very clear about this point. However, renegotiating a relationship can be a difficult process, particularly when outsiders are explicit and persistent in their questioning about the nature of the relationship. In addition, as the partners begin to date others, tensions may occur that need to be addressed. Teresa and Tony recognized the difficulties inherent in this process and were committed to managing them mutually. Most important, Teresa and Tony had been, and continued to be, patient with one another, for they understood that the redefinition process took time and effort.

Melissa and Bryan

Teresa and Tony attempted to manage uncertainty by talking about the relationship. In contrast, during periods of relational ambiguity, Melissa and Bryan chose to avoid talking about their relationship. They both responded to my question, "Do you avoid talking about anything?" by replying, "Us."

Melissa and Bryan differed in their perceptions of the type of relationship that they created shortly after they met. Bryan believed that they were dating at one point in their relationship, but only for a brief period of time. Melissa did not discuss this period in the interview, but instead said, "I never thought in a million years he would ever have an interest in me. So I just decided I'd be his friend." When I asked Bryan why Melissa and he did not continue dating, he said:

> "We got along a helluva lot better being friends than we did with being in a relationship or whatever. Um, and the main reason why we got along better being friends than in a relationship was that she was . . . it seemed like, when we were on a dating level, um, she was always seeing two or three other guys also. And that's just the type of girl she is. Just can't sit still."

During this period, Bryan gave Melissa money when she was unable to pay her bills and often sent her flowers, balloons, and stuffed animals. During her interview, Melissa mentioned all of these things, but stated that she did not interpret these behaviors as expressing romance. Rather, she thought that Bryan was being supportive as a friend. It was nearly 1 year later, after Bryan had expressed his feelings to her, that Melissa understood his intentions. Their misunderstanding about the nature of their relationship early on is a good example of the difficulties that Bryan and Melissa had experienced throughout the course of their friendship. Especially in the first 5 years of their friendship, they had experienced little agreement about its definition.

Both recalled one instance, while they were vacationing in Florida, when Bryan expressed his feelings for Melissa. Melissa was completely surprised by this and, as she said, did not react well to his declaration. She remembered:

> "For the very first time ever, he said, 'I love you. I've always loved you.' And to me 'I love you' is a really strong thing to say. I don't take it lightly at all. And I think that I was so hurt with the fact that I didn't know and he didn't tell me before. That wasn't what I wanted to hear, and I dealt with it wrong. And I'll always regret the way I dealt with it, but that was just my instinct at the time. Because I had no idea. I had no idea. And then it went away. It went away for 3 or 4 years."

Bryan remembered this period as being painful because Melissa broke off contact with him for several months. Similar to the incident between Linda and Chris that I described earlier, the interaction that Bryan described above created a "parametric disruption" (Bateson, 1991d, p. 61) in the relationship. In other words, the interaction engendered a "change in the very terms which define the system." (Bateson, 1991d, p. 61), which differs from the continuous change illustrated by the descriptions of the stabilized friendships. The stabi-lized relationships responded to various internal and external influ-ences "within the terms of the system" (Bateson, 1991d, p. 61), or within the context of a friendship. The change described by Bryan and Melissa and by Linda and Chris constituted an abrupt change in their patterns of interaction. In other words, as a result of a particular interaction, the "old rules" of their relationship no longer applied.

Because of this abrupt change, Melissa and Bryan did not see one another for several months. Upon meeting at a local bar, they acted as though the problem had not occurred and began what they both described as a "friendship" once again. Melissa described this meeting: "It was like nothing ever happened. I was so happy to see him and so happy to talk to him. It was, like, 'Let's get together.' 'Okay.' 'Cool.' It was weird."

For the subsequent 3 or 4 years (neither of the friends were clear on the time frame), Melissa and Bryan did not talk about their relationship with one another. During that time, they described their relationship as a close friendship. Both dated other people and talked about those relationships with one another. Melissa recalled that approximately a year and a half before our interview Bryan had asked her, "Melissa, have you totally given up on the thought of us?" She said she was "thrown for a loop," but that because this had happened once before in the relationship, she knew how to handle it better. Melissa described her response:

> "I think I was emotionally ready to handle it differently. That was the last thing I wanted to hear. But now, you know, over the 3 or 4 years, whatever it's been, that I've been through different relationships, I appreciate him differently. I think I always took for granted that he would always be there. And he was this person who was big and strong and never got his feelings hurt, and he was always the shoulder that I cried on. So I tried to be more sensitive this time."

Bryan reflected:

> "I do remember thinking, 'Okay, this is the last chance I'm giving the relationship.' And I started thinking if it doesn't go smoothly after this, then, you know, I'm not going to pursue it anymore. It seems like I can remember that I was going to give the relationship side one more chance and after that I wasn't going to pursue it. I didn't want to go through that hump again."

When it became clear to Bryan that a dating relationship with Melissa would not be possible, he realized that he wanted to keep a close friendship with her. He said:

> "I've learned to discipline myself and, um, that I would want to discipline the relationship to keep the friendship because I don't want to go . . . I'm going to discipline it to where it's not going to go into a relationship again and then crack off again, you see?"

When I asked if he was, seeking a more stable relationship, he responded, "Yes."

After the last incident, Bryan and Melissa again refrained from talking to one another—this time for a period of 6 months. However, as before, they had picked up the friendship once again as though the incident had never happened.

Bryan and Melissa's relationship had been difficult at times because of their inability to address mutually and directly the issue of romance. When one of them was interested in pursuing a romantic relationship, the other was not. As Melissa described it, their "timing" had been "off." Further, they were not able to talk about their relationship. Instead, they broke off contact, waited for the hurt feelings to subside, and then resumed their friendship.

Romance and Sexuality in Cross-Sex Heterosexual Friendship: Summary

In sum, my participants' descriptions indicate that concrete expressions of affection and intimacy between heterosexual men and women assume meanings within the context of a close friendship unlike the meanings that identical behaviors might acquire in a romantic relationship (Duck, 1994). Understanding the meanings placed on affectionate behaviors *by these friends* necessitates locating their friendship practices within their historical and social structures, tracing the friendships' development, and noting the friends' responses to changing configurations of internal and external constraints.

Romance and sexuality were deemphasized in the majority of the participating cross-sex friendships. For the remaining pairs of friends, romance and sexuality were not encouraged but did constitute salient ongoing issues in the friendship as the partners attempted to define the role that such feelings and actions would play in the relationship. Managing these issues is problematic, as my description of the friendships of Teresa and Tony and of Melissa and Bryan demonstrates. It also appears that the issues were managed in varying ways. Two modes were illustrated in this chapter: Teresa and Tony actively monitored their relationship, while Melissa and Bryan adopted a "together, then apart" strategy. In other words, when romance and sexuality became explicit issues in Melissa and Bryna's relationship, they disconnected their relationship only to resume it after a sufficient period of time had elapsed.

I urge researchers to explore answers to the following questions related to the management of romance and sexuality in friendships between heterosexual men and women: How do cross-sex friends discuss the issue of sexuality in their relationships with one another? What factors enter into cross-sex friends' decisions to become or to not become romantic or sexual partners? If the cross-sex friends do engage in sexual behavior, how does that activity influence the relational dynamics? How do the messages received from third parties influence the management of romance and sexuality in cross-sex friendships? The above questions are not exhaustive, but raise issues that have not been explored previously by cross-sex friendship researchers.

ROMANCE AND SEXUALITY IN FRIENDSHIPS BETWEEN HOMOSEXUAL AND HETEROSEXUAL PARTNERS AND BETWEEN HOMOSEXUAL WOMEN AND MEN

Cross-sex friendships in the homosexual community have rarely been researched. Existing studies have investigated same-sex friendships within the homosexual and lesbian communities (see Nardi, 1992; Nardi & Sherrod, 1994). However, friendships between the two communities remains unstudied. One form of cross-sex friendship that has received attention (although quite limited) is friendship between gay men and straight women. Conventional wisdom has been that friendships between gay men and straight women are common (Altman, 1982); however, the frequency of this form of friendship is not really known.

A recent survey conducted by Nardi (1992) indicates that gay male–heterosexual female friendships may not occur frequently since less than 10% of gay men in his sample stated that their best friends were heterosexual females while 82% of the men said that their best friends were gay or bisexual men. Nardi explains these numbers by citing the emergence of a gay-identified community where close relationships are forged primarily with other gay persons.

Other researchers (Malone, 1980; Whitney, 1990) have conducted studies specifically targeting the relationships between gay men and heterosexual women. This research has not been limited to friendships but also encompasses married and "committed" relationships. Paradoxically, both research projects reveal that although many of the participants viewed their friendships as a safe haven from the perils of sexual and romantic relationships initially, sexual attraction and activity between the friends existed. The people in these studies managed this attraction in different ways. A woman participating in Whitney's (1990) study summed up her frustration with this issue by stating:

> "I don't know whether my gay friend and I qualify as a 'gay-straight love match.' We're not lovers, but we do love each other, and it seems that there is some sexual energy between us that is disconcerting to us both. It has caused some problems between us, and I can't say with any certainty that we've come to terms with it yet, although we are both more comfortable with it than we were three years ago. Our relationship has survived a lot of confusion and frustration." (p. 115)

What is interesting about these results is that they question the assumption that sexual attraction occurs only in friendships between heterosexual men and women. In other words, these results defy dichotomous thinking about heterosexuality and homosexuality and suggest fluidity between the two concepts. These studies also suggest that the participants grappled with defining their relationships since their relational experiences stood apart from the "normal" man–woman bond. Much like the heterosexual cross-sex friends whom I have interviewed, these participants struggled with definitions of love, commitment, sex, and long-term relational goals.

Dichotomous thinking about sexual orientation may also be challenged by friendships between gay women and men. An interesting collection of essays about friendships between these communities, written by persons engaged in these friendships highlights the close and complex relationships between gay men and women (Nestle & Preston, 1994). These essays reveal the societal forces of oppression that propel gay women and men toward friendships with one another and expose the forces of sexism that drive a wedge between the two communities. Further, the writings of gay men and women about their friendships with one another uncover the sensual nature of cross-sex homosexual friendship. In this way, these friendship stories add further evidence questioning our heterocentric assumption that expressed or unexpressed sexual attraction occurs only between heterosexual men and women.

There is much to be learned about cross-sex friendships in the homosexual community as well as cross-sex friendships between homosexual and heterosexual men and women. Such study is worthwhile because ignoring these forms of cross-sex friendship truncates our knowledge of the diversity of norms, rules, and societal contexts within which men and women forge friendships (Duck, 1994). The following questions may be explored by researchers: To what extent does cross-sex friendship occur between gay men and women? What facilitates or impedes its formation? What issues are important in this form of cross-sex friendship? How do these concerns correspond with cross-sex friendship in the straight community? What is the nature of cross-sex friendship between homosexual and heterosexual persons? Is this type of cross-sex friendship viewed as somehow more legitimate by outsiders because this type of friendship is considered "definitively" nonsexual?

Again, the above questions and comments are meant to be generative in nature. In the future, researchers need to expand their investigations to include a wider variety of cross-sex friendship forms if they are to make valid claims about the nature of such friendship in American society.

CONCLUSION

The primary focus of this chapter has been to describe how men and women create close bonds in which romantic or sexual desires are not acted upon. After analyzing the interviews, I believe that the longevity and high level of emotional interdependence characterizing the stabilized friendships were possible because romance and sexuality did not present ongoing problems in the relationships.

If the negotiation of cross-sex friendship is to be understood, romance and sexuality are important topics for study since, from the perspective of my interviewees, this issue seems to be closely linked with the viability of cross-sex friendship (Sapadin, 1988; Werking, 1992, 1994b). However, investigations of these issues should not overshadow studies into other cross-sex friendship dynamics. As Rawlins (1994) suggests, let us "bracket" the issue of sex and pursue studies about other important relational dynamics, such as what cross-sex friends (of differing sexual orientations) do with and say to one another. In other words, as researchers, we must be cautious about reproducing a dominant heterocentric ideology in our studies (Rawlins, 1994).

5

The Public Side
of Cross-Sex Friendship

Managing Third-Party Relationships

KIM AND SHANNON

Kim, 25 years old, and Shannon, 24 years old, are white, heterosexual, college students, involved in dating relationships. They have been close friends for 3½ years.

Kim

> I can think of numerous specific examples of people comin' up to me and sayin', yk [you know], "So what's up with you and Shannon?" But . . .

Shannon

> Well, even at the bar the other night, when that girl thought I was hittin' on you, and I smiled and I told her I wasn't—that you and I are . . . it's the way that I say that, you know. People say I don't get defensive or anything, I just sort of smile . . .

Kim

> Yeah. *(laughs)*

Shannon

> . . . because I don't know. I don't deny it totally. It's not like I want to deny, 'cause then I would be like saying, "She's not my

friend, you know." 'Cause, you know, you're my best friend. In a way it's way beyond hittin' on you.

Kim

Right. Right.

Shannon

So when people say that, I just sort of smile because they're trivializing what it is. So I guess that makes it harder for people to believe that there's not anything going on, because I don't deny it.

Kim

Yeah. I follow that exactly because I suppose if both of us were, like, "No way!" you know, then they'd believe us. I don't know, I guess, you know, I'm very fond of you, and that's what people see when I say, "Oh, you know, we're just friends or whatever." I guess they see that, you know, 'cause people read what your . . . not only what the words are but the message behind the words.

Shannon

Yeah.

Kim

So, I guess if I didn't really care about you or whatever and I went, like, "Naw," then it would be different.

Shannon

I agree. When people ask me about you, I know I get that little . . . my eyes sort of . . . they light up.

Kim

(Laughs)

Shannon

You know, 'cause when I think about you . . . we really have fun. We laugh. You know, all we do is fun things, and, you know, yeah, I can't anything hostile or . . . I light up, and people probably read that the wrong way.

Kim

> Mm hmm. Then I guess it's actually *our* fault. You can't fault people for seeing that.

Kim and Shannon's conversation highlights the connection between cross-sex friendship and the larger social network insofar as the scrutiny of outsiders is one aspect of managing a close cross-sex friendship. This chapter presents a description of the public side of cross-sex friendship as described to me during interviews. In this chapter, I discuss the friends' management of several third-party relationships, focusing on the influence of these outside relationships on the cross-sex friendships and the friendships' influence on the third-party relationships.

THE PUBLIC SIDE OF CROSS-SEX FRIENDSHIP

As I have described it so far in this book, negotiating a friendship's "rules of relevancy" only regulates the private side of the friendship; it does not include rules for managing its public side (Paine, 1974). Cross-sex friends, therefore, face a second array of communicative tasks: negotiating the public image of their relationship.

These important and ongoing challenges for cross-sex friendship do not arise in a social vacuum. Instead, the friends' relationships with others affect the friendship in various ways, and their ongoing involvement in a cross-sex friendship influences their other relationships. The persons whom I interviewed described how diverse outside relationships were meaningfully connected to their cross-sex friendships. These "outsiders" included their families of origin, spouses, dating partners, other friends, and coworkers. In this chapter, I will focus on two outside relationships that notably shaped the practices of cross-sex friendships: relationships with the friends' families of origin and with the friends' marital or dating partners. I chose these specific relationships because they were mentioned most frequently by the people when I interviewed and because they seemed to be relationships that "mattered" to the friends.

CROSS-SEX FRIENDSHIP AND FAMILY

Since many of these friendships had a long history, throughout the course of developing and maintaining them the friends often came into contact with each other's families. Many of the friendships began when the friends were in high school together and were therefore still living at home. Likewise some grew out of a friendship one had had with the other's same-sex sibling. In situations where the friends happened to live a considerable distance from one (or both) of their families, one friend might accompany the other on visits home. It was even easier for one friend to get to know the other's family if one (or both) of the families lived nearby.

Nearly one-third of the pairs of friends interviewed reported that one of the pair enjoyed a close relationship with the other's family; however, in only one pair was there a close relationship between both friends and their respective families. As I read through their comments, it became evident that a number of these friends viewed their cross-sex friend to some degree as a member of their own family and that the family concurred in this sentiment. This was clearly indicated by the way the family integrated the cross-sex friend into their family life.

Family as Metaphor

When these cross-sex friends attempted to explain the nature of their friendship to me, they often used familial terms. For example, one man described his cross-sex friend as someone "who's almost as close to a spouse as you can get without getting married." Another person described her male friend as a substitute for her father after he had passed away. Her male friend echoed this idea when he asked, "Who's going to be able to take care of her?" as he attempted to explain his continuing commitment to the friendship. Others viewed their cross-sex friend as the sibling they did not have in their family of origin.

The most common type of familial descriptor used by these friends was "brother–sister," and their descriptions of their friendships were peppered with references to this sibling relationship. Interestingly, these labels were often used as a way of explaining their relationship to others. One man said: "I don't know, she's probably about as close to me as my sisters. You know, if anybody asked who it was if we were out together, I'd say, 'This is my sister.'" Another man stated:

"For example, we'd be in a group setting where there's someone new there, and we'd be talking, and then I would slide into a conversation like, 'Yeah, we are more like brother and sister, we have a lot of fun.'"

One woman said that she introduced her male friend as her brother to her friends:

"I call him my brother. I introduced him as my brother, because I don't have one. And when he goes up to a guy I'm dating and says, 'If you don't bring her home by twelve, I'm going to kill you,' I'm, like, 'Oh, God.' This guy walks in, and he sees this guy his own age in my house, and most people don't think that he is your brother. And I am, like, 'Well, he is sort of a friend, kind of a brother, father-figure person who looks over what I do. Kinda oversees everything.' And he's, like, 'Oh.' And he knows how to make things difficult if he doesn't like him. He's done that. If he doesn't like the guy I was dating, he would make things very hard. Just 'cause either he's obnoxious and acting like a brother, or, I don't know, I could belt him."

Another woman tells outsiders that her friend is her adopted brother. She said:

"Yeah. He's our adopted brother. That's what I told this little girl that started working for me: 'He's my adopted brother and he comes and stays with us. We love him as a brother.'"

Yet another woman stated:

"A true friend is like someone who is there for you when you need them or don't need them. And just someone whose honest and, you know, like a brother or sister to you. And with Ted it's more like a little sister type of thing and, um, you know, kind of taking care of me."

Each pair of cross-sex partners had experienced questions from outsiders about the definition of their relationship. The questions usually focused on whether or not the relationship was a romantic one. Employing a brother–sister metaphor as a means of explaining cross-sex friendship to perplexed or suspicious third parties was plausible because these cross-sex friendships displayed many of the trappings of a brother–sister relationship. The sibling relationship is an enduring bond between a male and a female that is void of sexuality. This label also allows for friendly relations between a male and female because a close sibling relationship may include a wide variety of behaviors, some of which may contain elements of friendship (Paine, 1974). The label is useful as well because kinship is an institutionalized relationship with guidelines for behaving and interpreting behavior between related persons, thereby assisting outsider's understandings of the relationship.

Integrating Cross-Sex Friends into Families

Viewing the cross-sex friend as a family member was also evident in the language used by friends and family members in describing their relationships. Parents called their offspring's friend "son" or "daughter," and the friends referred to the other's parents as "Mom" and "Dad." In addition, expressions of affection and love were commonplace when discussing the relationship with family members. One woman said her mother is "just nuts" about her male friend. Debbie stated that she gets along very well with Alex's parents and that his niece and nephew "love her to death . . . I'm an aunt." Her friend confirmed this perception by saying, "My mom and dad love her. She gets along great with my niece and nephew." These themes were also echoed in this woman's comments about her cross-sex friend's relationship with her family:

"He calls her Mom, calls my dad, Dad. They treat him as a son. He comes over for dinner when I am not even home. And we slept in the same bed that night, and she's, like, 'Well, that's nice.' She doesn't care. My mom is not like that. I am not allowed to have guys in my room. So Rob and I sleeping in the same bed is like . . . that would be death in my house if it was anyone but him."

This comment clearly illustrates the acceptance of this cross-sex friend as a member of the family. Behavior that would be unacceptable by someone whom the parents viewed as a romantic partner or even a close male friend is considered acceptable when the relationship is defined as a "brother-sister" relationship. In fact, several pairs of friends had slept in the same bed while traveling or while moving into a new apartment. All of their parents knew about it, and none were concerned. Instead, it had become the source of jokes among family members. One recurring joke in Ron's family was that "Ron and Phyl have slept together in five different states."

A further indication that these friends were considered "family" is that they were included in family celebrations, such as Mother's Day and Christmas, family dinners, day-to-day activities, and family crises. Joyce's brother, Dave, asked Todd to visit their mother on Mother's Day 2 years ago because Dave couldn't be there. Todd said that Dave asked him "to be the brother that's not there for my Mom and the family." Since then, Todd has continued to spend Mother's Day with Joyce's family.

In addition to sharing the joys of family life, the cross-sex friends have been asked to assist during times of family crisis. Ron was asked by Phyl's mother to be a pallbearer at the funeral of Phyl's father. Phyl remembered her appreciation of her mother's request and talked about that as being an important moment in her friendship with Ron. Nan also told of the day when she learned of her biological father's death. Nan had not been in contact with her father and knew little about him, but was overcome with grief. Confused, she turned to Ed for comfort, and both of them talked to her mother about never-discussed issues surrounding her mother's divorce.

For several of the friends, however, the process of integrating a cross-sex friend into their families involved certain difficulties. Initially, parents were skeptical about whether the relationship was a friendship and asked their son or daughter about it. For example, when I asked Debbie about how her friendship with Alex influenced her family relationships, she replied:

"The only turmoil that was caused was when Mom wasn't sure where Alex and I's relationship was. But Mom understands. Mom's finally understood what our relationship is and stuff."

Many of the cross-sex friends experienced similar scrutiny from either their parents or siblings. Several partners responded to this scrutiny by explicitly telling their families that the relationship was "just a friendship" or that "there's nothing going on between us." Others simply ignored the questions and hoped that they would cease with time. Whatever the strategy, once the family members' curiosity was satiated, they welcomed the friend into their home.

Even so, two friends indicated that although their parents accepted each friend, they believed that the parents harbored a secret wish that the relationship would develop into a romance "just because they liked him" or because "he's that person that you need." One man believed that his friend's parents would approve if he and his friend started dating: "I don't know, she'll even say to this day that . . . that her parents are kind of attached to me or whatever. I don't know what the right words would be." When I asked whether his friend's parents considered him to be a good prospect for a boyfriend, he responded:

"Yeah, I guess so. I mean, she would openly say that she would even use me towards her parents as far as, you know, she'd say, 'Oh, I'm going out with Tad tonight,' or something like that. Well, they'd just perk up. (Laughs)"

During their taped conversation, June told Greg about her family's expectations regarding their relationship:

June

My stepmother thinks we're going to get married.

Greg

Oh, really? That's pressure right there.

June

Yeah, she's had dreams that you and I got married.

Greg

She's not a soothsayer, is she?

June

No, no. Just wishful thinking.

Tensions with Family Members

The integration of one friend with the other's family of origin also created potential tensions among family members as the friend developed relationships with them. Two women, each of whom had a sister, talked about how their sister had become very jealous of the time they spent with a male friend because the jealous sister too had developed a friendship with him. Further, the women both recounted times when arguments over the issue had erupted with their sisters. The women's male friends were aware of the conflict and spoke ambivalently: they felt quite uncomfortable yet also complimented that the sisters feuded over them. One male friend said, "You kind of like the attention, but then you don't really like the conflict it creates. It will always be a conflict." The other spoke of feeling as if he were being "pulled in two directions."

Other friends talked quite positively about the relationships they had developed with their friends' family members. One man saw his cross-sex friend's brothers "all the time" and said that they often would "have beers together." His female friend also viewed his friendship with her brothers as being very pleasant, although she did foresee problems in her friendship with him if he and one of her brothers "got into it." In another dyad, the man spoke very highly of his female friend's sister and stated that he had turned to her for advice during times when his cross-sex friendship was teetering between friendship and romance.

In sum, the participants' discussions about their involvement in the lives of their friends' families focused primarily on the positive aspects of this involvement. These "family-type friendships" were seen as enriching, but they were also viewed as potentially problematic because of an increasing number of relational obligations. Although they viewed their cross-sex friendship as their primary relationship, they did not discount the responsibilities inherent in their relationships with members of their friend's family.

Involvement with a cross-sex friend's family also created tensions within one's own family of origin. Two dyads talked extensively about the problems created in their own families because of the time they chose to spend with their friend's family instead of their own. One man stated:

"They may be a little jealous just because they know it's more of a family-type friendship than just a friendship. There are tensions with my family as far as how close I am with her. Just jealousy. I can think of what my sister would say: 'Okay, it's the same distance whether you come down to see me or come up here [to see her family].' It's always much easier up here than it is with my family. (Laughs)"

This man had spent Christmas with his cross-sex friend's family instead of with his own 2 years ago. When I asked him how he felt at that time, he said: "Guilty. They laid guilt on me. And I felt guilty too. Kind of torn between, you know, the friendships and also the family."

Another man had also experienced difficulties with his family over his cross-sex friendship. He described these difficulties:

"My parents didn't like it at all. My mother just doesn't understand how I can have this relationship and . . . I think they view it as taking time away from them. That's what they do. That I would want to spend time with my friends and not with them."

His friend knew about the problem and shared this perspective on the situation:

> "His parents are, um—I don't know if I want to say jealous—perturbed with me. Because he always wants to come here. I know he told me they made a comment because he said he wanted to come up and see me, and it's, like, 'Well can't she come to our house?' It's, like, 'Well, it's not the same,' you know. So I . . . as far as his parents go, there's envy."

When I asked the male friends what they did to manage their family's jealousy, each said that many times he did not tell his parents when he would be visiting his friend and her family. Even though both men felt guilty about the situation, they believed that maintaining silence was the best strategy for avoiding confrontations.

Family as a Subject of Talk

Cross-sex friends' familiarity with partners' families of origin resulted from involvement *in* family life and from talking with their friends *about* family life. Their respective families were a major subject of talk among these cross-sex friends. The content of this talk included gossiping about the family, retelling family stories, discussing family crises, and working through problematic family relationships.

When I asked these friends what they talked about with one another, one male responded:

> "We gossip a lot. About family members. Either my family or her family. The relationships between. I guess our relationship is almost a given: 'We're fine. These other people are not doing so well.' "

His female friend also cited their families as a topic of talk. She stated:

> "We floated on the pond when he was home Memorial Day. We talked about his family and his sisters and his relationships with

them—his true sisters. We talk about our family. You know, we pick people apart. We talk about Joe [her husband]."

Another woman interviewee responded to my question as follows:

"We gossip about my family. *(Laughs)* We talk about our families a lot. You know, he's not real close with his parents, and I think he's real envious because I am real close. And so I think he likes to hear stories about my family 'cause we all, you know, even though we bitch about each other, we're all real close."

In these friendships the roles of "friend" and "kin" were often fused. At times, however, the separation of these roles allowed for the exploration of family dynamics with someone other than a family member. Such role separation facilitated the frank discussion of family issues in which the cross-sex friends received the perspective of someone who was simultaneously involved in and removed from family life.

Talking through family problems, particularly about major family issues such as the death of a parent, the divorce of parents, or illness in the family, brought several of these cross-sex friends closer together. I asked the friends to describe times when the one felt particularly close to the other. In response, they related stories about one helping the other through the death of a family member or the divorce of his or her parents.

The persons whom I interviewed also described talking about the day-to-day management of family relationships as influencing their attitudes and behavior toward other family members. Such "relationship management talk" did not stand out in the interviewees' minds as vividly as talk about family crises. Still, they did cite several instances where their friends had influenced how they related to family members, particularly their parents. For example, one man believed that he was more nurturing in his relationship with his mother because of his cross-sex friend. A woman remembered when her friend had helped her understand her mother's perspective in a disagreement. Another man recalled times when his cross-sex friend regulated his behavior with his family because she was not afraid to tell him that he was acting inappropriately.

The Functions of Talk about Families

These accounts of talk about families shared similar characteristics. Specifically, in talking with their cross-sex friends, these men and women were able to analyze family situations and mull over various courses of action. And this process was facilitated because their friends were well acquainted with the problematic relationship but were detached enough to be less biased in assessing the situation. In addition, talking about family seemed to strengthen the bond between these cross-sex friends for, at times, grave family situations arose that required the cross-sex friends' support. Finally, on a more mundane level, the sharing of family successes, problems, and gossip allowed the cross-sex friends access to each other's lives and contributed to mutually developed and richly textured conversations between the friends.

Although there were instances where the boundaries between friendship and kinship blurred for my participants, there also were times when these friends drew sharp distinctions between a friend and his or her family. The unique qualities of friendship, reciprocity, and equality contributed to an openness with friends that generally was not found with family members. In addition, an important dimension of friendship is acceptance. Typically, friends bring a nonjudgmental perspective to situations, whereas family members are more likely to judge behavior (Rawlins & Holl, 1988). The acceptance that she had experienced in her friendship with her friend led a woman to say:

> "I'm really close to my sisters and my mom and dad, but I'm even closer to him. I tell him things I would never even tell my family. He's always been there for me, and they haven't always. When they haven't understood something that I have done, you know, they've hurt me. He never has. Whether it was right or wrong, he was there, you know."

The above interview excerpt exemplifies the openness of these cross-sex friends because they had proven their availability and acceptance of each other's behavior—behavior that may occasion hurtful responses from family. For example, several of these interviewees felt comfortable discussing with their cross-sex friends aspects of their lives that they were reluctant to discuss with their families. Personal topics, such as romantic relationships, were identified as topics that they would share with their friends, but not with their own families. Activities that they knew would not receive family approval, such as drinking or drug use, were also not discussed with their families, but were shared with their friends.

Cross-Sex Friendship and Family: Summary

The cross-sex friends' relationships with their families of origin situated these friendships within a network of relationships that posed a range of communicative dilemmas. As a family embraced a cross-sex friend, there was an opportunity for developing relationships with other family members. Seizing this opportunity both enriched the cross-sex friendship and subjected it to a host of new dilemmas. Specifically, tensions arose when family members felt left out of friendship activities or when a friend felt that the friendship was being neglected for the sake of the family relationships. Potential problems also existed with the involved friend's family of origin since that family may not understand the nature of the cross-sex friendship or the family member's involvement with the cross-sex friend's family. Lastly, participating in a friend's family of origin provided an opportunity to become more fully involved in the friend's life through sharing family celebrations and crises and dealing with family problems.

Because of its unique status in American culture, friendship may fuse with, compete with, substitute for, or complement other social relationships (Hess, 1972). The experiences reported by my interview participants provide examples of friendship's capacity to function in all of these roles. Ongoing cross-sex friendships were viewed as familial relationships at times and as sources of family tension at others. By and large, however, these cross-sex friendships seemed to affect positively the friends' relationships with family members and provided support for the friends during periods of family turmoil.

I have discussed the cross-sex friends' relationships with the families of origin. For the married friends whom I interviewed, another important member of the immediate family was the spouse. I now turn to addressing the issue of managing a close cross-sex friendship when one member of the dyad is married.

MANAGING CROSS-SEX FRIENDSHIP AND MARRIAGE

Marriage exerts a profound influence on the development and maintenance of friendships. As people move through adulthood, their responsibilities to spouse and children typically overshadow their obligations to friends (Rawlins, 1992). Results of studies investigating same-sex friendship and marriage point to this reality as contacts with friends diminish after marriage (e.g., Milardo, Johnson, & Huston, 1983). Studies investigating cross-sex friendship and marriage also show a decline in the number of friendships after marriage. However, marriage seems to affect cross-sex friendships to a much greater degree than it does same-sex friendships (Block, 1980; Booth & Hess, 1974; Rose, 1985; Rubin, 1985). Given the above research results, it seems that being involved in a close cross-sex friendship while married poses challenges that are difficult to overcome.

I conducted 19 of 100 interviews with married persons. The majority of my married interviewees were women; only three were married men. Therefore, I will provide primarily the female perspective on managing cross-sex friendship and a marital relationship. I do include, however, the male friends' perspectives on the process as well as the comments of the three married men.

As I studied their words, it became clear to me that successfully managing a separate cross-sex friendship while married requires *improvisation*. Improvising involves "recombining partly familiar materials in new ways, often in ways especially sensitive to context, interaction, and response" (Bateson, 1989, p. 2). Improvisation involves risk, for the improvisor sees what is created only as it is completed; the particular shape of the creation cannot be predicted.

Married persons involved in cross-sex friendships are on unfamiliar terrain. There are many models for composing a marriage, as there are for engaging in same-sex friendship while married. However, none of these female and male friends described models from which to work. Neither their parents nor their married peers had served as models. Finally, their spouses did not have close cross-sex friends. In short, these women and men were crafting relationships without a clear vision of how to proceed. In the following sections, I present the ways in which the friends whom I interviewed managed potentially problematic situations and the ways in which their cross-sex friendships and marriages informed and opposed one another.

The Effects of Marriage on Cross-Sex Friendship

Of the 16 married women whom I interviewed, 14 of the friendships had been established before the marriage, whereas the three men had been married prior to the establishment of the cross-sex friendships. Because the friendships existed before marriage, the married women and their friends were able to talk with me about the changes that had occurred within their friendships as a result of marriage.

All of the friends felt that the new marital relationship took priority over the established cross-sex friendship. Many of the women spoke of difficulties fitting their friends into an overburdened schedule. Several strategies had been used to overcome these difficulties. In some instances a pair of cross-sex friends would dine with their spouse and the other friend's dating partner. One pair set aside one morning a week to get together and drink hot cocoa and watch the morning talk shows. They chose this time because the woman's children were at school and her husband was at work. This dyad also reserved one evening a week to go out for a drink. Both friends mentioned that these rituals offered little spontaneity in their friendship, but ensured that they would continue to spend time with one another. Other friends did not encounter the issue of finding time to spend with one another on a day-to-day basis because they did not live in the same city. When they did spend time together, it was usually a weekend-long visit at the other's home every 2 or 3 months.

Several of the women said that being married influenced their friendship in subtle ways. One of these changes was that the woman was less dependent on the friendship. As one woman stated:

> "I think in one sense it's because a lot of things I needed him [her friend] for, I don't need him for anymore. I have my husband who . . . it was just easier to go to Will, start going to Will for things"

Her friend had also noticed this change and commented:

> "And when a woman gets married, it changes the relationship because a lot of things that they will tell you or confide about and that sort of stuff is now to their . . . they need to do that with their husband if that relationship's going to survive. And so, that changes the relationship."

In four cases, the types of activities done with the woman's cross-sex friend changed after her marriage. These activities, such as going to see a movie, were avoided because the woman was concerned that outsiders might misconstrue their actions. One woman stated that she was very careful not to be in situations with her male friend where it might look as though they were dating, so they usually got together with mutual friends and went out as a group.

Cross-Sex Friends and Spouses

Married couples usually develop "couple friendships" (Babchuk, 1965; Bell, 1981a; Hess, 1972). However, since 18 of the 19 friends of the participating married persons were single, their cross-sex friendships were fairly independent of the married friend's spouse. None of the women believed their husbands to be overly concerned with their involvement in the friendship. But, one of the married men stated that his wife was very uneasy about his cross-sex friendship:

"We [he and his friend] would go out to dinner, uh, with my wife's knowledge. Not that she was happy about it. She was, you know . . . no, she never said anything.

"Until 5 years ago, we really had some problems. Karen and I nearly divorced. And, uh, Sarah [his friend] happened to come back to town, but we talked a lot. My wife and I went to a marriage counselor, and one of the things that came up was that she was upset because I could talk to Sarah and I couldn't talk to her. And she was jealous because of it."

The second man whom I interviewed said that his wife was very accepting of his friendship and made many gestures to be friendly to his female friend. The third man stated that his wife had never expressed concern about his 13-year friendship, and, since he and his cross-sex friend lived in different cities, he did not feel a need to integrate his female friend into his family life.

Even though the women and two of the men whom I interviewed said that their spouses did not voice concern, they carefully and continually monitored their spouses' feelings about the matter. Overall, the married friends' monitoring involved: (1) encouraging the spouse and the cross-sex friend to become aquainted, (2) being open with the spouse about the friendship, and (3) addressing the perceptions of the public-at-large. I will elaborate on each of these strategies in the following sections.

Encouraging a Positive Relationship between Spouses and Friends

Fifteen of these women had encouraged their male friends and their husbands to develop a good relationship. Usually, the male friend was invited to the female friend's house or arrangements were made to dine out with the friend. Oftentimes the male friend brought a date. Through these experiences, the spouses and male friends usually developed a positive relationship. As one male friend observed:

"Her husband and I are very good friends also. It's great, you know. I call up, and we chat for a little while, and then he puts her

on the phone. When I go over, the kids all tackle me, you know.
So, it's very comfortable. I know a lot of males who are very
uncomfortable with that."

How a cross-sex friendship develops appears to contribute to a
lack of tension between a spouse and a male friend. For example,
several friendships developed as a result of the man's being friends
with the woman's brother. Because of this preestablished friendship,
spouses viewed the potential for romance as minimal.

In other circumstances, it might take time for the male friend and
the spouse to become compatible. For example, at the time of the
interview, one man enjoyed a positive relationship with his friend's
husband but stated that it had only been in the past 3 years that he felt
her husband was becoming friendlier toward him. When I asked him
why he believed this to have happened, he replied that over time his
friend's husband had gotten to know him better and had become
more secure in his marriage. The male friend also believed that his
cross-sex friendship was more "tolerable" because he and his friend
lived in different cities and did not spend much time together.

The relationship between the spouse and male friend can become quite close. One woman's then-fiancé asked her friend to stand
up with him at their wedding. She described how she felt about their
blossoming friendship:

> "It feels good to know that he likes my husband so much. And
> that it's . . . because it would be very hard to know that, let's say,
> for some reason he and my husband didn't mix. That would just
> . . . that would be really tough. I mean, obviously, I would be with
> my husband, but, God, I would have hated to make a choice."

As the descriptions illustrate, the male friends in these situations
have been fairly successful at establishing friendly relationships with
the females' spouses. The female friends also seemed grateful for this
success, for, as the above comment highlights, the problems posed by a
threatened spouse might be too difficult to overcome and therefore
doom the cross-sex friendship.

Talking about the Cross-Sex Friendship

Although these participants described establishing successful balances between their friendships and their marriages, the connections between the two relational types have required, and continue to require, nurturing from all of the involved parties. All of the women said that they tried to be very open with their spouses about their cross-sex friendship, with their spouse, talking about what she and he did together and their feelings about one another. Moreover, the women recognized that the situation demanded their husbands' trust and understanding. In addition, both friends monitored their behaviors, such as the amount of time they spent together and their activities, so that their interactions would not be misconstrued by the spouse. Finally, both friends respected the primacy of the marital relationship and conducted the friendship around marital obligations.

In order to illustrate the precariousness of this balance between marriage and cross-sex friendship, I offer an extended section of my interview with Melanie. The situation discussed in this excerpt centered around Melanie's desire to travel out of town with a woman friend to visit Don, without her husband Jerry. Don had moved from Melanie's town 9 months prior to our interviews. He was involved with theater and was appearing in a play that was to take place approximately 1 month after the time of the interviews. Melanie had talked with her husband about her desire to see Don's play but her husband was feeling uncomfortable about her visiting Don. She related the following:

Melanie

It still is. It's not a daily or weekly discussion, but it comes up. I want to go out and visit badly. And that's a problem.

Kathy

Jerry doesn't really want you to do that?

Melanie

Um, no. And he says it's financial. You know, why spend the money.

Kathy

But you believe that it's something else?

Melanie

Yeah, I sure do. And that's hard. You know, then it feels like he's not trusting me. But if I think through and think, "Now would I want him to be friends with a woman and go visit her?" I don't know. Well, it's kinda hard to think about what we would do. Yes, I hope I could be understanding because I know how my relationship with Don is, so I would hope he could have the same kind of relationship.

Kathy

So, how did you approach Jerry about the visit?

Melanie

Oh, I said, "I wanna go and see it." I was assuming it could happen, and that was a wrong assumption on my part. I should not have made that assumption. I mean, you know, he's never kept me. I think that's why it was so difficult for us. Um, maybe I've never asked. He's never kept me—quote, unquote—personally or professionally, whatever. And sometimes it's a great hardship for him. I mean most music things—rehearsals—are at night. So he's been real understanding in those terms. But I don't know if he's worried how it looks to everybody else. Does anybody else really need to know? Not as far as I'm concerned. And I said, if it was just him or his folks or my mom that were worried, we could talk to them about it.

(Later in the interview)

Melanie

It's easier for Jerry to accept my friendship with Marilyn [her best female friend], I think.

Kathy

She's your closest friend to you?

Melanie

Yeah. Um, she's . . . we can go see her. If I were asking to go see her, he would not hesitate. The financial problems would disappear. Would disappear. No, he would probably mention it, but it would not be a deterrent.

(Later in the interview)

Kathy

Can you think of anything that might cause it [the friendship] to end?

Melanie

I don't . . . I don't know. We'll see how we get through this negotiating me going out. It could be real interesting.

Don was aware of the difficulties that this situation posed for Melanie. When I asked him whether or not he thought she would be able to visit, he said:

"She's trying to work that out with Jerry and that sort of thing. There's a . . . you know, people talk. In a small town like that . . . you know, 'Where you goin'?' 'Oh, we're goin' out to New York to see Don.' 'Oh, yeah?'"

Even though Don and Jerry were friendly with one another, Melanie's visiting Don pushed the limits of acceptable behavior, from her husband's point of view and therefore unsettled the negotiated relationships. Perhaps the act symbolized a commitment to the friendship that Jerry found unnerving or, as Melanie and Don have suggested, "how it would look" to outsiders became too great a concern. I can only speculate because I did not have the opportunity to speak with Jerry about the issue. The point, however, is this: *the actors in this situation had not been faced with such an issue previously and were uncertain about how to proceed.* They, therefore, had to improvise a solution—one that allowed the marital partners to continue to define their relationship as one based on trust and openness, that allowed the males to maintain a friendly relationship, and that allowed the cross-sex friendship to continue to flourish. In this case, Melanie and Jerry were able to achieve such a solution. Several weeks after our interview, Melanie called me to tell me that she was going to visit Don with one of her close female friends.

Managing Public Scrutiny of the Cross-Sex Friendship

In addition, the above excerpt highlights another important aspect of negotiating a cross-sex friendship and a marriage: successfully handling the public's perceptions of the friendship. These friends tended to say that they disregarded outsiders' perceptions and often joked and laughed about those perceptions with one another. Even so, they were keenly aware of outsiders' scrutiny and worked to minimize its effect on both their friendships and their marital relationships. The women also were concerned about their husbands' feelings about outsiders' perceptions of the friendship.

All of the married friends had experienced direct questions from third parties regarding the nature of the cross-sex friendships. A man said that when he went to lunch with his female friend everyone in his workplace teased him about having a lunchtime affair and asked him what his wife would say if she knew. One of the friends remembered some direct questions:

> "She was at a party last night, and people asked, 'Is she your girlfriend? I always see you guys together.' 'What does your husband think about him coming?' or 'What do you guys do?' or 'Why have you stayed friends for so long?' and 'Are you having an affair?' Some of the employees I work with, they're, like, 'I can't believe you do things like that.' They are so surprised that I am so open about my friendship in front of my husband. I guess everyone thinks of the sexual connotation, and there's really not one."

One woman also said that people had approached her husband about the friendship:

> "It's just like, 'What do you think about your wife runnin' around with this guy or whatever?' People that don't know me are very, 'I

bet your husband doesn't like him staying there.' *(Mimics other person)* And it's, like, 'Well, I don't think it really bothers him. You know, it's not an issue.' "

As I indicated previously, the friends tended to disregard these questions and did not feel that the questions had influenced the closeness of their friendships. The females said that they were able to ignore the questions of others because the only perceptions of their cross-sex relationships that they were concerned with were their husbands'. As one woman said, "As long as he [her husband] knows what's going on, I don't care about what others think."

The *awareness* of outsiders' scrutiny, however, had led the friends to ponder their feelings about the friendship, as illustrated in this comment:

"It . . . it has made me examine it. Certainly not change it, but look at it. Look at it in a different light. That maybe people think, 'Gosh, you're always there.' That kind of thing. 'Why am I always there? Why are you up there with a husband and wife? Don't you feel odd being up there?' And it's, like, 'No.' "

Hal discussed one period in his friendship with Maggie when they almost dissolved their friendship because of the scrutiny of outsiders:

"We had a problem at one point where people started trying to define us as an item. Which was, uh, not good for either one of us. First of all, I was married. And second of all, she has sort of a religious bent to her, and she didn't like the idea of people thinking that she was carrying on with a married person. So we sort of . . . I think at a point we sort of gave way to what other people thought and didn't see each other and didn't have much to do with each other.

"But it became silly. When people started seeing us as an item, it was a problem for us. But we were together a lot. I mean that that perception was a valid one. I could see why people would think that. I remember having a conversation with her after a few weeks of not seeing one another about how *stupid* this was. That people thought this. And how stupid *we* were for letting this have anything to do with how we wanted to carry on. We basically said, 'Screw it. We're going to do what we want to do.' And that's what we did. And that's what we still do."

An awareness of the "generalized public," brought on by outsiders' questions, prompted the friends to manage strategically the public images of their friendships. For example, I stated earlier that cross-sex friends reported altering their activities in order to minimize public concern about their relationships. One woman said that prior to her friend's latest visit she had talked with her male neighbor and explained that a male friend was coming for a visit and told her neighbor that if he saw another man at the house he should not be concerned. In response, the neighbor asked her a series of questions about her friendship and her husband's response to it. Last, a male friend said that when new people joined their group of friends he interjected into the conversation stories about his cross-sex friendship so that the newcomers' potential questions would be laid to rest.

These cross-sex friends had negotiated a close relationship that was publicly visible. As a result, negotiating a close cross-sex friendship while married took place against a backdrop of public scrutiny, which heightened the complexity of maintaining both relationships and added to the uncertainty of the task.

Despite these exigencies, the friends whom I interviewed had been reasonably successful, and the continuing existence of the cross-sex friendships spoke to this success. Still, simultaneous involvement in a close cross-sex friendship and a marriage require *work*. The difficulties inherent in the project were nicely summed up by Melanie, who responded to my question, "Could you see yourself being friends with a married man?" in the following manner: "Hmm. Hmm. Um, gosh, no, not in the same way. Because then we get two, *two* spouses. I think that could be real stressful."

The previous discussion has pointed to areas where it might be construed that cross-sex friendship and marriage are mutually antagonistic. Indeed, there are tensions to be addressed when participating in both relationships. I also found, however, a very strong opinion among these friends that their involvement in a cross-sex friendship strengthened the marital bond. I now turn to a description of this positive influence on the marital relationship.

Cross-Sex Friends and "Marriage Work"

My participants echoed Oliker's (1989) finding that female best friends perform "marriage work." She defines "marriage work" as "reflection and action to achieve or sustain the stability of a marriage or a sense of its adequacy" (Oliker, 1989, p. 123). The marriage work of female friends involved listening to marital problems, suggesting solutions, offering criticism, and probing emotions. One result of engaging in marriage work with a female friend was a heightened commitment to the marriage.

In the accounts I heard, cross-sex friends also engaged in marriage work. Though the nature of the marital work may have differed somewhat from that done in same-sex friendships, it did not undermine the marital bond, as has been suggested by other researchers (e.g., Francoeur & Francoeur, 1977; Lampe, 1985), but reinforced it.

These cross-sex friends performed marriage work when they talked about marital relationships and spouses. Several male friends said that their female friends often talked to them about problems in their marriages many times before they talked with their husbands about them (if they talked over the problems with their husbands at all). The male friends believed that when problems were discussed, their married friends walked away with possible solutions or insights into problems. Thus, friends saw their cross-sex relationships as a positive influence on marriage. One woman stated that one of the biggest rewards of talking with her male friend was that he provided a different perspective on the situation. She said:

"If you are having a difficult time understanding your relationship with your spouse, another male can say, 'Well, now wait a minute. You know, he's not so far off. He sees it this way.'"

Another woman testified to the importance of talking over problems with her male friend:

> "Getting to see what the other side is like. *(Laughs)* You kinda think, you know, see how the men think about things. You know, I won't get that out of my husband. But I will hear that outta Bob."

According to all of these married interviewees, and to several of their cross-sex friends, it seemed that involvement in a cross-sex friendship lessened the emotional burden placed on the marital relationship. This relief was an important way in which the cross-sex friendship nourished the marital bond. Emotional burdens were diminished because the married person was able to experience the companionship of the opposite sex, gain the opposite-sex perspective, and share similar interests with a member of the opposite sex without experiencing romantic involvement or encompassing marital responsibilities. Consequently, these interviewees did not expect their spouses to fulfill their emotional needs to the extent to which they might have expected if their cross-sex friendships did not exist. Further, these men and women recognized that there were aspects of their lives that their spouses were not interested in or that their spouses were unwilling to share with them. The married women also believed that it was healthier to share those things with male friends than it was to continue to heap expectations on their spouses. A woman expressed this awareness nicely when she stated:

> "And I've often said that I feel like there are two halves of me. This mother–wife half that my husband gets and then the music half that my friend gets. There is . . . no, my husband cannot understand that. He loves me dearly, but there is just . . . he can't share that. I mean, that is just not a passion of his.
>
> "Just like figuring out how things grow is not a passion of mine. That's the difference and that's fine, but it is a passion. I can turn to my friend and say, 'God, did you hear that in the music?' And I look over and he's crying too. And that's an immediate emotional link that I can't share with my husband."

One man saw his cross-sex friendship as enabling his marital relationship to continue:

> "I can talk to her [his friend] about things I can't talk to my wife about. In fact, because I have her friendship, I can continue my marriage without expecting to talk to my wife about everything. And that's good, because there are some things I shouldn't talk to my wife about—even though I love my wife more than anything in the world. Telling her certain things might hurt her feelings or make her think less of me. My marriage is *better* because of my friendship."

In addition to providing emotional support or the opportunity to share interests, these cross-sex friendships also provided a break from the everyday routine of marriage. One man characterized his role in his friend's marriage as providing a "diversion from everyday life." Similarly, another man spoke of his friendship as giving his cross-sex friend a "break" from her marriage. A woman said that with her cross-sex friend she did not have the "financial crap . . . the kid crap . . . the in-law crap." Cross-sex friendship was viewed by these interviewees as an arena in which they could have fun and receive emotional support, which ameliorated marital demands as it rounded out their interpersonal lives.

Cross-Sex Friendship and Marriage: Summary

For the most part, the positive influences of engaging in a close cross-sex friendship while married have been overlooked. My interviews with close cross-sex friends not only point to the beneficial contributions that cross-sex friendships can make to marriage but also begin to uncover cracks in the assumption that cross-sex friendship subverts marriage. This negative assumption was clearly reflected in the questions that outsiders asked these friends. Yet, it was within such a context that these cross-sex friends had to orchestrate their relationships. Their task was not easy. It was filled with tension and ambiguity and required ongoing effort and commitment from the involved parties. These friends, however, seemed committed to trying to "make it work" even though they were aware that it might not. This awareness was clearly reflected in their responses to the question, "Can you think of a reason that would cause your friendship to end?" *All* of the participants cited their spouses' objection to the friendship as a possible reason.

I now turn to my participants' experiences in reconciling their dating relationships and their close cross-sex friendships. I noted many similarities between the comments about marriage and about dating relationships. Though closely aligned, however, there were divergences stemming from the differing privileges and obligations inherent in each relational type. Thus, the management of each relationship constituted a distinctive communicative task.

MANAGING DATING RELATIONSHIPS WITH THIRD PARTIES

I interviewed 81 unmarried cross-sex friends. All of these friends had been involved in a romantic relationship with a third party at some time during the course of their cross-sex friendships. The dating relationship was the most frequently mentioned problematic third-party relationship. This man's description of his girlfriends' responses to his cross-sex friendship is a typical description of the problems posed by romantic partners:

> "My girlfriends, the ones that I've had, have always kind of resented her 'cause I'd rather hang out with her than them sometimes. I mean she doesn't get mad at stuff. I had a girlfriend that would call and say, 'I'm going to come visit you tonight.' And I'd say, 'Oh, I'm going out with Sheri.' And she'd get mad. But Sheri and I are just friends. I give her priority over going out with other people 'cause we always have a good time when we go out. We're always laughing and joking and having a nice time. And that's not usually the case with my girlfriend. I mean, they are always jealous of her. Sheri's good-looking and all, and they

always think the worst. 'Oh, you guys are fooling around.' *(Laughs)*"

This man suggested that the jealousy or discomfort felt by an outside romantic partner stemmed from his cross-sex friend's strong presence in his life. Bringle and Buunk (1985) define jealousy as any negative emotional response "that occurs as the result of a partner's extradyadic relationship that is real, imagined, or considered likely to occur" (p. 42). The prototypical jealousy-evoking extradyadic relationship is sexual or romantic in nature (Bringle & Boebinger, 1990). Thus, a person's romantic partner may construe the activities of a cross-sex friend as threatening.

Indeed, the friends whom I interviewed reported spending a great deal of time together, often by themselves, watching movies, talking, eating, or "just hanging" out together. They also turned to one another as confidant(e)s, telling each other their problems and gaining insight into those problems by receiving the perspective of the opposite sex. Such closeness posed a threat to romantic relationships since romantic partners felt excluded or interpreted these behaviors as "dating behaviors." This perception is reflected in the following observation by an interviewee:

"I dated a guy for 2 years, and he was just so jealous of my friendship. He thought it was just so intruding that I could talk to Joe as closely as I could talk to him, and that kind of caused problems."

A recently divorced woman discussed how her 10-year cross-sex friendship needed to be "explained" to her new romantic partner:

"I was married for a number of years and so didn't carve out new romantic relationships with anybody during that period of life. And, um, the friendship preceded the romantic relationship with my spouse, and so it was just always sort of a given. "Ok, so she's got this friendship with Larry. They were involved before, but they're friends now." So, it was always kind of a given. Um, so there really weren't questions there.

"I think with the new romantic partner, um, there probably are more questions in his mind, um. I think they're pretty much worked out. But I think I've gotten more questions from him because he really doesn't have much of a history of being close friends with women, so it's, um, an anomaly to him. And, um, again we haven't known each other that long and so he hasn't seen . . . you know, he hasn't had a good deal of time to see my pattern of rela—, friendships with men."

Other reasons for jealousy included the attractive physical appearance of the friend and the romantic partner's opinion that close friendship between a man and a woman while either was dating another person was "wrong" by definition. This assumption was clearly evident in my survey of people who did not have close cross-sex friends since many participants pointed to their involvement in a romantic relationship as the primary reason for not having a cross-sex friend (Werking, 1994a). These participants often believed that the dating partner also should be the best friend; thus, it was inappropriate for the partner to engage in a friendship with a member of the opposite-sex.

A romantic partner's concern about the cross-sex friendship may ultimately lead to the breakup of the romantic relationship. A few interviewees cited their involvement in the cross-sex friendship as the reason for dissolving a romantic relationship. A woman described her feelings about possibly being forced to make a choice between the person she was dating and her cross-sex friend:

"But if it came down to . . . if I had to decide . . . if I would ever have to decide between my friendship and my relationship with Ron, you know. Men have come and gone in my life, you know, and Scott has always been there, and I would definitely have to . . . I would sacrifice any relationship that I had with a man for the friendship that I have with him. Definitely."

These words portray a theme underlying many of these friends' comments about the differences between cross-sex friendship and the dating relationship: *the cross-sex friendship was viewed as more secure than the dating relationship.* The interviewees also believed that the cross-sex friend would "be there" for them—a belief that was not expressed when describing the more volatile dating relationship. These differences parallel the findings of other social scientists who have described romantic partners as less understanding, less accepting, and less tolerant than close friends (Davis & Todd, 1982).

I do not want to overstate the occurrence of the romantic partner's jealousy. Many people did report that their present romantic partners were very tolerant of their cross-sex friendships. This tolerance often evolved over time as the romantic partner became more secure in the dating relationship or realized that "nothing was going on" between the friends. For example, Chad stated:

"Well, she [his girlfriend] was jealous at first. But I've had a lot of female friends. But she doesn't care anymore because she trusts me. She knows that I'm . . . that there's certain things I get out of a relationship with Lisa that, you know, that I get out of my relationships with guy friends. You know, there's nothing there to be mistrustful of."

Although many friends stated that their romantic partners were not threatened by the cross-sex friendship, other friends reported that they carefully monitored the situation for a time because they wanted to avoid potential problems.

What was striking about the discussions of romantic partners was that *all* of the friends alluded to the *potential* for problems with their dating partners because of their involvement in a close cross-sex friendship. Because this potential existed in their minds, they engaged in two contrasting types of preventative strategies: either openness or closedness about the cross-sex friendship.

One strategy for monitoring the situation was talking with the dating partner or the friend's dating partner about the cross-sex friendship early in the dating relationship. One man said that he was just "straight up" with his friend's boyfriend. When one woman began a new dating relationship, she explained her cross-sex friendship to her romantic partner in the following way:

> "I did that forthright. As soon as Daniel and I became 'very good friends,' I said there's another guy in my life, and I explained the whole thing to him. And he's, like, 'Well, that's cool.'"

Other friends withheld information from their dating partners to avoid their partners' jealousy of the friendship and to avoid confrontation. Past experiences had informed many of the friends that openness did not work as a preventative strategy. As a result, oftentimes cross-sex friends would give minimal information about the time that they would spend with their cross-sex friends, or they lied to their dating partners about where they were going or who they would be with.

It should be noted that neither the openness nor the closedness strategy was always successful in laying to rest the romantic partners' fears about the cross-sex friendship. In some instances, an initial strategy of openness met with failure, and so the friend adopted the strategy of closedness in order to "avoid creating problems." Such was the case with Melissa's current boyfriend Pat. When she first started dating him, she introduced him to Bryan and encouraged them to spend time with one another. Pat resisted and argued with Melissa whenever she spent time with Bryan. As a result, Melissa stopped telling Pat about her activities with Bryan.

Perhaps the friends' awareness of the potential problems posed by close cross-sex friendship was best revealed in their expressed desire to find someone to date or marry who would understand the cross-sex friendship and not be threatened by it. Each of the relevant participants either applauded their romantic partner for not being threatened by the friendship, or they clearly hoped that their future romantic partners would be comfortable with the friendship. A woman summed up her feelings regarding both points: "And he [her boyfriend] accepts it. Daniel accepts it quite well, and that *means a lot to me. I will not marry anyone who does not accept my relationship with Alex"* (emphasis hers). One man stated that his future romantic partner would need to accept his cross-sex friendship: "I'm sure it would cause some problems, but, uh, just . . . I guess we are such good friends that people we go out with will just have to understand that's all we are—just friends. We like to spend time."

Cross-Sex Friends' Talk about Dating Relationships

There were many similarities between the cross-sex friends' conversations about marital relationships and dating relationships. Much like the "marriage work" that strengthened the marital bond, the nonmarried cross-sex friends also provided assistance in managing dating relationships.

Getting the Perspective of the Opposite Sex

Talking about both real and imagined romantic relationships constituted a primary activity. These friends turned to each other for advice about problems that they were experiencing with their current dating partners. One of the reasons cited for doing this was that they could get a different perspective on the problem from their opposite-sex friends. In essence, they felt they could get more fully inside their romantic partner's world by talking with a person of the same sex as their partner. A sampling of their comments on the value of this follows:

> "Girls can get together if you're . . . whether you're, like, in a serious relationship or just going out with someone, you get down about things. And you talk to your girlfriends, and they feel the way you feel. And then you talk to your male friends, and they're, like, 'Well, wait a minute. Take a step back and look at it. Maybe what he said he meant this, or he meant this, or he meant this.'
>
> "Someone who can give me like a male perspective on a problem. If I, um, if I'm having like a relationship problem with

my boyfriend, I can talk to my friend about it . . . and he's, like, 'Well, lighten up, or you were in the wrong, or he was in the wrong.' They can give me kind of a male . . . a male viewpoint.

"Well, if you're dating a girl, and we're having a fight, and I'll share it with my female friend, and she'll give me an insight from a female perspective on things. The male view of the world is very different than the female view of the world, and so you can get an additional perspective from the female.

"I guess you can like say you have . . . like you've got girl troubles, they can help you on how girls would feel on certain things, like what girls like."

As these comments demonstrate, obtaining a different perspective on relational problems is a benefit of having a close cross-sex friend. It seemed that in situations where misunderstandings arose between romantically involved men and women, the benevolent nature of a cross-sex friendship offered these persons a forum in which greater understanding could be achieved.

By offering support and a listening ear, these cross-sex friends had also been there when romantic relationships ran awry. Consistently, the friends whom I interviewed referred to this availability and assistance at several points in their interviews. Many of the interviewees had experienced sudden breakups with their romantic partners during their friendships. According to the interviewees, their cross-sex friends' support was what helped them put their lives back in order afterward. This restoration was accomplished by talking for hours on the phone or by enhancing their friends' self-esteem by pointing out their positive attributes. Many friends referred to these times of crisis as periods when they felt very close to one another.

Talking about romantic relationships also seemed to influence the friends' behavior or thinking concerning future romantic relationships. One woman stated:

"He and I have talked an awful lot about what he wants in a spouse. You know, What do you want? And saying it, you know, making him look at what he wants. Is it realistic? Is it not realistic? So in many ways it will have influenced his future relationship."

In addition to talking explicitly about future relationships, other friends said that they learned a great deal from listening to their friends' relationship experiences, learning vicariously what to do and what to avoid in romantic relationships. One man said that one of the most valuable lessons he learned from his woman friend was the following:

> "I always want . . . I always want to openly talk about things. And you can do that with friends, but you cannot do that with someone you are having a relationship with. There's just times to keep your damn mouth shut. And that's what I learned."

Avoiding Talk about a Dating Partner

Although romantic relationships and partners were frequent topics of conversation, at times these topics were selectively avoided. Avoiding talk about the romantic partner was practiced in many of these friendships, but for differing reasons. First, several of the friends had dated or were currently dating a person who was also a friend of the cross-sex friend (many times that was the way the cross-sex friends met each other). Because of the close connection between the involved parties, the friends refrained from talking about the romantic relationship. One woman talked about avoiding the subject of her ex-boyfriend in the following way:

> "We avoided talking about my ex-boyfriend at the time because he was still kind of friends, but he knew that was a touchy area with me. And so we really . . . I think there were times that we mentioned it, but we really just didn't talk about that. Anything else . . . I mean, he is just one of those people that you could just tell whatever to."

As described in a previous section, some of the friendship dyads had previously defined their relationships as romantic or had experienced difficulty managing the romantic aspect of their friendships. Many times these cross-sex friends adopted a protective stance toward their partners and bypassed discussion of their romantic interest in other people. One woman stated:

> "We just felt uncomfortable with each other for a while after we stopped dating and were friends again. We didn't feel comfortable talking about what happened between us or about our involvements with other people. After a time we started talking about the people we were dating, but we still don't talk about the time when *we* were dating."

Tensions also arose in these friendships when one friend disliked the other's romantic partner. Friends usually are very accepting of each other's behaviors; however, people also expect friends to be critical of behaviors that they strongly feel are negative or not in a person's best interest (Rawlins, 1989a; Rawlins & Holl, 1988). Expressing criticism may be quite difficult, however, particularly if it is directed at a person whom the friend is dating.

Accordingly, these friends hesitated in voicing their objections about a friend's boyfriend or girlfriend or about a friend's behavior with a dating partner. Yet, for the most part, when objections were voiced, the person who was being criticized accepted the friend's opinions. However, a few friends described instances when their friend responded defensively or angrily and said that it took some time to repair the friendship. In one instance the friendship waned for 2 years until the woman broke off her romantic relationship. After the breakup, the cross-sex friendship "flourished" once again. The man involved in this friendship said about the boyfriend of his cross-sex friend:

> "He was a jerk, a jealous type, and I didn't like being around him anyhow. But I honestly didn't like being around her when she was dating him just because I thought she was a different person. When she stopped dating him, that opened the door for us to have a friendship again. So then we resumed our friendship."

Managing Feelings of Neglect

In addition to providing a prevalent topic of conversation for these friends, either friend's romantic involvement with another person could directly affect the closeness of the cross-sex friendship. According to their remarks, friends felt "neglected" when a friend had a dating partner. When I asked one man to recount times when he felt distant from his female friend, he stated:

> "The last time we went out, she pretty well contacted me. Um, I knew that she was seeing a lot of somebody. And there'd be a few times when we would kind of lose touch for a while because her time was occupied with who she was seeing. But when it would go to shit, my phone would ring."

A woman also talked about a time when she felt disappointed with her male friend:

> "Um, he kind of got involved with a girl, and he neglected me, I guess you would say. It wasn't so bad at first, you know. I understood. He really liked her and wanted some time. And then he stopped seeing me to see her, and he stopped telling me he wasn't [going to see me]. Like, we would have plans, and he didn't tell me that all of a sudden she had called and he was going there. And we got into a fight about that."

As the participants talked about their romantic relationships juxtaposed with their cross-sex friendships, their words echoed the priority given to romantic relationships in this culture. I have already discussed the priority given to marital relationships, and it seemed that an analogous status was granted to dating relationships as well.

Because of friendship's marginalized status in American society (Rawlins, 1989a), a same-sex friendship is often forsaken when a person enters a romantic relationship (Milardo et al., 1983; Rose, 1984; Weinstein, 1982). For these participants, it also appeared that cross-sex friendships took a back seat to romantic relationships. Even if the friendship itself was not threatened, its emotional closeness was strongly and negatively correlated with either friend's involvement in a romantic relationship since the romantic partner diverted the friend's attention and time away from the friendship. A woman recognized this reshuffling of her priorities after she began dating her current boy-friend:

> "Once you're . . . I feel like I'm committed to a person [her boyfriend], the only time I have free is on weekends, and he's the person that I guess I choose to spend time with. That's terrible."

When I asked her if she had made that a higher priority, she responded: "Yeah, I guess so. I hope that doesn't sound bad." Robert also described the effect of dating relationships on his friendship with Sue:

> At first, after she . . . well, when she was going out with Mike still, my friend? It was pretty close then, and I'd see her a lot. And then when her and Mike broke up, I was kinda like upset over it. And when she got a new boyfriend, I didn't talk to her at all that much. I was pouting or something. But then we got closer again. And then I got a girlfriend, and I was busy. And so after I broke up with mine, and, uh . . . and then we got closer after I broke up with my girlfriend."

The primacy given to romantic relationships by these friends may be considered ironic because the participants typically described their cross-sex friendships as being more supportive, accepting, and stable than their romantic interests. In addition, several of the friends held their cross-sex friends in higher esteem than their romantic partners and explicitly said so. Even so, their romantic relationships were given priority over their friendships.

Managing Third-Party Dating Relationships: Summary

In this section we have seen that cross-sex friends' romantic relation-ships with third parties modified the character of the cross-sex friendships and vice versa. In the extreme case, either or both relationships may have been threatened. At the very least, involvement in these relationships posed communicative dilemmas for the friends, such as dealing with a romantic partner's suspicions about the "true" nature of the cross-sex friendship, addressing the friends' feelings of neglect when one or both of the cross-sex friends were involved with third parties, and sensitively handling criticism of the friends' romantic partners.

CONCLUSION

In the social sciences, we tend to observe things in isolation. By and large, researchers have maintained a focus on individuals or on the internal dynamics of specific relationships (but see Duck, 1993). However, maintaining this focus obscures the linkages among relationships.

In contrast, the above discussion of these cross-sex friends' relationships with third parties more fully situates the friendships in their social context. Such a conception begins to uncover the tensions inherent in the practices of cross-sex friendships in conjunction with the practices of relationships connected to them. I focused on three relationships—families of origin, marriage, and dating—because, from the perspectives of the men and women whom I interviewed, they were the most salient relationships.

The friends whom I interviewed have woven their cross-sex friendships into many areas of their lives. For the most part, these friends were directly or indirectly involved in a friend's family of origin, in a marriage, or in a dating relationship. Their participation in these spheres enriched the cross-sex friendship as their range of potentially shared experiences expanded. Meanwhile, their participation in the cross-sex friendship often enhanced these other relationships as well, as the friends developed heightened understandings of family members and/or the opposite sex. Moreover, the cross-sex friendship itself occasioned a set of new life experiences for the participants' family, marital, or dating relationships.

What I found most striking about the friends' descriptions was that their participation in multiple relationships did not necessarily "take away from" any of the relationships, but instead complemented them. In other words, for these friends, participating in multiple types of relationships did not constitute a zero-sum game in which being involved in one relationship detracted from the others. Instead, as they simultaneously cared about and managed multiple relationships, the friends continually created new relational forms and practices that responded to real and anticipated problematics. This process was most evident in the friends' descriptions of their management of a close cross-sex friendship while married. As the cross-sex friends became closer to one another, they coordinated their activities with an awareness of their interconnection with the actions of affected marital partners. Consequently, they created new ways of "being friends" and new ways of "being married."

Perhaps this interconnection of relationships is especially salient for cross-sex friends because of the cultural status of cross-sex friendship in this society. As described earlier, cross-sex friendship does not neatly fit into a widely accepted or clearly defined relational category. While creating and maintaining a relationship in such a cultural climate, these cross-sex friends were aware of how their actions could be interpreted by outsiders, and this awareness was clearly present in their descriptions of their cross-sex friendships.

All of the friends had experienced questions from outsiders regarding the nature of their cross-sex relationships. In the present cultural context, third parties to cross-sex friendships experience and communicate an interpretive quandary: Can a male and a female negotiate a close bond, based on trust, affection, and loyalty, without it being or becoming a romantic relationship? The questions posed to these cross-sex friends by acquaintances, relatives, coworkers, friends, and lovers reflected this quandary. And these questions served as continual reminders to the cross-sex friends that their private practices had a very public dimension. As a result, if the cross-sex friends were unable to orchestrate a public image of their relationship that others would interpret as a "friendship," then their unceasing responses of doubt and suspicion could eventually undermine the viability of the friendship.

The analysis of these interviews point to a wealth of future research projects focusing on the interconnections between third-party relationships and cross-sex friendships. One strategy for learning more about these interconnections is to interview the involved third parties. For example, gathering the marital partners' perceptions of their spouses' close cross-sex friendships and the friendships' effect on the marital relationships would be particularly intriguing.

In addition, the connection between cross-sex friendships and romantic relationships demands further investigation. My participants described clear distinctions between their cross-sex friendships and their romantic relationships and often idealized their cross-sex friendships while scorning their romantic relationships. These descriptions point to another possible avenue of research for exploring the variations in behavior, expectations, and perceptions of heterosexual romantic relationships and cross-sex friendships.

Finally, my interviews uncovered a relatively unexplored friendship issue: the connection between friendship and family. Thus, future research could address such issues as the following: How are cross-sex friends integrated into family life? What are the dimensions of family life from which cross-sex friends are excluded? What aspects of the cross-sex friendship are "off limits" to the family? When are cross-sex friendships viewed as substitutes for family relationships? Investigating these and other questions will strengthen our insights into the management of cross-sex friendship.

Conclusion

DIANE AND ANDRE

Diane, 22 years old, and Andre, 24 years old, are heterosexual, single, college students. Andre is African American, and Diane is white. They have been close friends for 1 year.

Diane

Our friendship is special or unique probably because I've never had a friendship this close where I've bonded with somebody so close and I haven't been their girlfriend. Um, you're totally unique. You're one of a kind in good and bad ways! *(Both laugh)* Um . . .

Andre

I guess what's unique about it is . . . I mean it's just . . . we have so much in common, yet we come from so completely, totally different backgrounds. It's just weird. Sometimes we just think the exact same thing, and sometimes we are just completely in two different states. And I don't . . . it's just . . . it's weird because you know what I like a lot of times, and, like, I know what you like. And just . . . we can be completely mad or upset or pissed off about something, and then we'll see each other, and you'll get to tellin' about something that you did or something that happened today, and, I mean, it'll just cheer me up.

Diane

> And because half the time stuff we do is not anything, I mean, we'll just sit there, and we'll start havin' a water fight or wrestlin', all that kind of stuff. Somethin' that nobody else would think was any fun, but we just get kicks out of it just 'cause we enjoy each other's company so much.

Over several years of research, my studies of cross-sex friendship illustrate clearly that cross-sex friends can care deeply for one another—in many instances "love" one another. This love, however, is not synonymous with romantic love. Rather, it is a love rooted in mutual respect and symmetrical rights and obligations—in short, friendship. Skeptics often question the possibility of a close cross-sex friendship that does not result in the friends' becoming lovers. Indeed, friendship is seen as the ideal basis for developing a romantic relationship. Further, a strong emotional attachment between women and men is frequently seen as deterministic in that it overwhelms the partners' abilities to make thoughtful judgments about what type of relationship is appropriate for them (Raymond, 1986).

My work and the work of others contests the prevailing assumption that close, affectionate ties between women and men necessarily evolve into sexual or romantic relationships. My analysis of the existing data suggests that as cross-sex friends negotiate how their relationship is to be defined, they simultaneously negotiate the role of romance and sexuality within that definition. As they create a relational definition, friends consider the circumstances of their lives, such as their commitments to others, and incompatible personalities, life goals, or sexual preferences.

Indeed, some cross-sex friendships *do* become romantic relationships, but not *all* cross-sex friendships evolve into romance. Those friendships that do not segue into romance transcend prevailing assumptions about what man–woman relationships ought to be like. Through the process of transcendence, cross-sex friends confront and manage what has been described to me as "almost palpable" judgments and expectations not only of specific individuals in the friends' social networks but also of "society" in general.

My work has, in large part, focused on the challenges inherent in the management of these judgments and expectations. There are, however, many rewards associated with having a close cross-sex friend. The benefits of cross-sex friendship are similar to those associated with same-sex friendship. Cross-sex friends offer comfort during difficult times, an outlet for the expression of fears, feelings, and fantasies, companionship, acceptance, and greater self-knowledge. Cross-sex friendship also offers a reward that is not available in the context of same-sex friendship: a window into the world of the other sex. According to my own and the research of others, cross-sex friends help one another explore problems and offer insight into how a cross-sex party may be perceiving a given situation. As a result, cross-sex friends report a greater understanding of their cross-sex romantic partners, employers, coworkers, parents, and siblings.

For the friends whom I have studied, the sometimes different perspectives brought to the friendship by men and women were celebrated and respected. A man expressed this component of cross-sex friendship in the following manner:

> "The word *friendship*. I would say that it's either . . . there's two types of friendship. There's two people that have a lot in common, and there's two people, like my cross-sex friendships, that are really . . . they're not opposites, but they enjoy spending time with each other because they are different. They enjoy each other's experiences or each other's ways of looking at things."

In addition to gaining the perspective of a cross-sex person, man–woman friendship also provides the opportunity for women and men to interact in innovative and unconventional ways. The friendship invokes the possibility that a relationship between a man and a woman can be based on equality, affection, intimacy, loyalty, trust, and reciprocity. Thus, men and women may overcome their homosocial and sexist tendencies as they forge friendships with one another.

The unconventionality of cross-sex friendship may be its greatest weakness, as well as its greatest strength. For as men and women construct new modes of relating, the novelty renders the relationship vulnerable in many ways. First, third parties' lack of understanding threatens the viability of the friendship. Second, persons do not have agreed-upon ways of talking about woman–man platonic bonds. The cross-sex friends whom I interviewed demonstrated this clearly as they struggled to express their feelings about their cross-sex friend to one another and to outsiders. Thus, cross-sex friends must invent a language by which they construct new meanings in novel private and public situations. Until such a language is created and widely employed, cross-sex friendship will continue to be viewed as a deviant relationship.

Finally, cross-sex friends do not have adequate role models and must therefore improvise much of the cross-sex relationship. The risk is that in an ambiguous private and public context, the friends may fall back on the closest culturally defined woman–man relationship—the romantic relationship—as the basis for their interpretation of the friendship (Lampe, 1985). In other words, the friends themselves may succumb to the heterosexual romantic ideology and begin to view their bond as romantic or sexual in nature.

The men and women who have participated in research studies have provided glimpses into the management of cross-sex friendships and the possible forms of platonic man–woman relationships. These friendships are not alike; each dyad addressed unique sets of personal and social involvements and expectations for friendship (Rawlins, 1992). There are, however, many common themes coursing through the studied friendships. My goal has been to identify those themes in the work of other scholars and in my own work.

A second goal of this book was to incorporate these themes into a theoretical framework in order to "make sense" of existing research results. This framework provides a language for talking about the internal dynamics of cross-sex friendship as well as the cultural and societal context within which cross-sex friendship takes place. In this way, the framework differs from existing research because it shifts the focus of study from the individual to the dyad, the social group, and the wider culture within which cross-sex friendship is enacted. It also departs from existing cross-sex friendship research because the framework creates a way for addressing issues of process, struggle, and constraint as cross-sex friends respond to forces inside and outside the cross-sex relationship.

I utilized the framework in two ways in this book. First, I organized existing studies within the framework so that the reader would have ready access to one interpretation of the "history" of research into this topic. Second, I presented the results of my own work in order to demonstrate how the framework may inform actual research. While the framework provides the metaphor for guiding research, within its parameters there are many specific choices to be made by the researcher. I describe some of the choices I have made below because I rely extensively on my own work in this book.

During the course of my studies, I made several methodological decisions—choices that profoundly influenced the nature of the information that I shared in this book. First, I chose to generate grounded descriptions of the everyday experiences of close cross-sex friends by conducting in-depth interviews with pairs of friends and by analyzing these data qualitatively. These data then informed the surveys that I conducted since the surveys gathered information about topics that had been discussed in the interviews but that had not been investigated previously. In this way, I hoped to capitalize on the strength of combined qualitative and quantitative methodologies.

I also made decisions about which aspects of cross-sex friendship I would present in this book. The framework sketches numerous possibilities for intensive study; however, I chose to develop those themes that seemed most important to my interviewees and to the participants in work conducted by other researchers. These themes are not exhaustive of this sample nor of the themes that might be evidenced when other types of people are included in studies. This is the nature of interpretive projects; they are "unfinished business" (Duck, 1990). This does not mean that conclusions are not offered; it does mean that the interpretive process is ongoing and begins anew each time a researcher returns to the phenomenon (Denzin, 1989).

I did not start my research into cross-sex friendship believing that I would come to know everything that can be known about the close cross-sex friendships under study. The choices that I made opened up some areas for illumination and closed off others. For example, I limited the discussion of potential cross-sex friendship experiences by developing standardized interview protocols and survey questionnaires. By so doing, I imposed order on my participants' experiences. I did, however, develop these questions as a result not only of reading the existing cross-sex friendship literature but also of conducting exploratory investigations. Further, I have talked with hundreds of people on an informal basis about cross-sex friendship in the past 5 years. That has been one of the delights of my chosen topic of research: academics and nonacademics are fascinated by the topic and are eager to share information from their lives. My research questions and the questions included on my instruments grew out of these activities, and in this manner I attempted to remain sensitive to the voices of cross-sex friends. Nevertheless, the protocols and questionnaires remain my organizational scheme, not my participants' scheme, for the experience of close cross-sex friendship.

I also made choices about who would participate in my research. As a response to the existing literature that rarely limits the type of cross-sex friendship under study, I imposed several restrictions, such as duration and closeness of the friendship, on the types of cross-sex friendships eligible for participation. Because of these criteria, I caution readers about generalizing my descriptions of these enduring, close cross-sex friendships to other types of cross-sex friendship. Inferential limitations are also posed by the characteristics of my participants. My samples have been composed primarily of relatively young, middle-class, heterosexual, white, educated women and men. Cross-sex friendships enacted by other age, racial, and sexual-orientation groups within varying socioeconomic conditions may differ dramatically from the experiences that I have related in this book.

The above decisions occurred throughout the research process and concerned the nature of my sample, the development of my research instruments, and the presentation of my results. The two most critical decisions that I made, however, were the decisions to include both partners of the dyad in my research and to tape-record the friends' conversations with one another. Gathering information from both partners through individual and dyadic interviews provides rich data. Further, it allows for the examination of the ways in which the descriptions correlate with one another. Because the friends cocreate the cross-sex relationship, inclusion of their perspectives brings us nearer to their shared relational reality (Rawlins, 1992).

Tape-recording friends' actual discourse provides further insight into their shared world. Even though I had talked extensively with my interview participants about their cross-sex friendships, I realized, when confronted with the task of examining their conversations, that I had not completely entered their friendship worlds because I had not experienced their *talk*. Listening to their conversations enriched the impressions that I had formed during my interviews with them because I could "see" in the talk their descriptions "in action." Through these conversations, I witnessed the friends' affection for one another, their enjoyment of one another, the struggles and concerns that they had about their relationship, and the enmeshment of their lives as they talked to *one another, not to a third party,* about themselves, friends, family, future plans, past events, and work. I urge scholars to incorporate this type of data into their research.

By writing this book, I have sought to "extend the conversation" (Rorty, 1979) about the management of cross-sex friendship by organizing existing research, providing a conceptual framework, and offering cross-sex friends' descriptions of their relational practices. Cross-sex friendship is a relationship ripe for study. My hope is that the information presented in this book will ignite the reader's thinking about cross-sex friendship and will stimulate imaginative strategies for theorizing and conducting research. There is much to be learned about cross-sex friendship, and there are many ways to become more knowledgeable.

Appendix A

Methods of Research

I. Interviews with Pairs of Cross-Sex Friends

Description of the Sample

I conducted intensive, open-ended interviews with 50 pairs of cross-sex friends. The participants were primarily white, middle-class, heterosexual adults between the ages of 21 and 46. Five of the participating friends were homosexual. The length of the friendships studied ranged from 1 year to 17 years. My sample consisted of 81 single and 19 married persons. The participants were well educated since all of them had continued their education past high school. Three of the participants had earned doctorates, 10 had earned master's degrees, and the rest had attended or graduated from college. The participants were involved in a variety of professions, as managers, teachers, military officers, salespeople, and business owners.

Resembling previous research by Rawlins (1981), to participate in this study, the friends met five requirements: (1) their relationship was defined primarily as a friendship, (2) both partners considered their relationship to be a "close" friendship, (3) they had to have been close friends for at least 1 year, (4) both had to appear interested and involved in the friendship and willing to talk about it, and (5) both had to be willing to make the time commitment that was necessary for the study.

I obtained participants through personal contacts. I asked friends, neighbors, family, students, and university faculty and clerical staff for the names of persons whom they felt would meet the above criteria for participation in the study. In general, the persons recommended to me were interested in participating in the study. However, I was unable to interview several dyads because they did not live in the same geographical area.

Interview Procedures

The interview protocol questions (see Appendix B) were derived from Rawlins's (1981) study of friendship, Bolton's (1959) research on courtship, and Baxter's (1987) investigation of relational symbols. Additionally, I developed questions specifically related to the goals of this project.

Each friend was interviewed individually, using the standardized interview protocol. I attempted to schedule each dyad's interviews as close together as possible to reduce the opportunities for the friends to discuss the interviews. Scheduling problems did arise at times because of the busy lives of the participants. It was particularly difficult to schedule the dyadic interviews. In fact, I was not able to conduct the dyadic interview with nine of the friendship dyads because of scheduling problems.

I conducted the majority of the interviews in the friends' homes. Several interviews were also conducted in my office. Typically, the interviews were between 1½ and 2½ hours in duration. An oft-heard remark made by the participants as they reflected upon a question was, "I never thought about this before!" Even though I asked them about aspects of their friendships that they had not pondered previously, their answers were typically insightful and rich in detail. I believe that the participants regarded the interview experience as a positive one.

Each interview was recorded on audiotape. After each individual interview, I studied the recordings to identify issues and themes in a friendship that were mentioned by both partners. These issues provided the basis for the dyadic interviews. It should be noted that after studying the recordings of three friendship pairs, I made the decision not to conduct dyadic interviews with them. There appeared to be extremely sensitive issues present in each of these friendships; I was concerned that talking about a relationship with both partners present could potentially instigate an emotional encounter between the partners that neither of them wanted.

The dyadic interview involved presenting both partners with a list of three or four mutually identified issues in their friendship. The partners were then asked to select two issues that they wished to discuss. I asked a set of questions (see Appendix B) about the history of each issue, about the effect of both issues on the friendship, and about the partners' management of those issues.

A second component of 32 of the dyadic interviews was asking the partners to converse for 10 minutes after I left the room. I made some suggestions about topics that they might wish to discuss, such as when they met or how their friendship compared with their same-sex friendships. As with the individual interviews, the dyadic interviews were recorded on audiotape.

Analysis of the Interviews

My analysis of the interview data began during data collection. Immediately after each interview, I recorded my reflections about the interview, asking myself such questions as the following: (1) What was my relationship with the interviewee? (2) What were my thoughts on the meaning of what was said in the interview? (3) What issues should be pursued further in our next interview? (4) What connections could be made with other interviews previously conducted? and (5) What were my feelings about what was said in the interview? The responses to these questions were recorded in a notebook and were referred to during later analyses.

After completing the interviews, I transcribed the audiotapes, noting relevant nonverbals, such as (1) tone of voice, (2) stress placed on certain words, and (3) pauses. Upon transcription, I listened to the tapes again to check for accuracy of the transcripts. Next, I read through the transcripts in their entirety several times.

During the analysis of the interviews, I treated each friendship pair as an individual case as I first constructed a history of each friendship by identifying and juxtaposing events discussed by both friends in chronological order. During this construction, I compared the partners' responses in order to ascertain key events or issues in the relationship. My goal for developing these descriptions of each friendship was to provide a context for the friends' comments about their relationship. In addition, after identifying the important themes, issues, and events for each dyad, similarities and differences could then be drawn across friendship dyads. Therefore, each friendship's unique aspects as well as recurring themes in several cross-sex friendships were identified.

After the descriptions of the friendships were constructed, I extracted and indexed statements from the transcripts relating to themes and issues that were evident across the dyads. Particular attention was paid to the interview responses about potential problematic concerns in the the relationships, such as sexual attraction, romantic interest, and third-party relationships.

After the relevant statements were identified, they were placed separately on index cards. I attempted to extract the statements in coherent wholes, including the questions that gave rise to the statements and pertinent information that I believed helped to preserve the meaning of the statements. Upon completing the archive, I compared and contrasted the statements with each other to identify unifying and differentiating themes. This process involved repeatedly reading and sorting the statements until groupings of statements emerged. These categories were then labeled, and the relations among categories examined. Periodically during this process, I again read through the transcripts in their entirety in order to remain close to the context in which these references were made. Finally, after the categories were refined, I chose segments of the interviews that illustrated the categories.

To date, I have limited my analysis of the dyadic interview data to the cross-sex friends' recorded conversations. I first read through each of the conversations several times to familiarize myself with their content. Next, I listened to the recordings themselves and then reread the transcripts. I did this for two reasons: (1) to check for the accuracy of the transcripts, and (2) to listen for paralinguistic features of conversation, such as tone of voice, rate of speech, and stresses placed on particular words or phrases. I then noted such features on the transcripts.

As I studied the transcripts, I initially looked for an overall focus of each conversation. After deciphering this focus, I then identified subthemes, such as particular friendship issues, in each conversation. When all of the conversations had been analyzed in this manner, I compared the identified themes across conversations in order to recognize commonalities and differences.

Finally, I compared the identified themes with the themes that I had extracted from the individual interviews, investigating the ways in which the conversations corresponded to the descriptions of each cross-sex friendship obtained in the individual interviews.

II. Interviews with One Partner of a Close Cross-Sex Friendship Dyad (Werking, 1994c)

For this study, in-depth interviews were conducted with 90 persons (50 men and 40 women) who were involved in a close cross-sex friendship at the time of the study. The ages of the participants ranged from 18 to 40 years (mean age = 23.2 years). I obtained interviewees through contacts made by my students in a research methods class at a Midwestern, urban college. The participants were primarily white (85%), heterosexual (100%), single (100%), and college educated (87% had attended some college).

The interviews lasted approximately 1 hour and each interview followed a standardized protocol. For the results reported in this book, the following questions were analyzed: (1) How do your opposite-sex friendships differ from a dating relationship? (2) How are your opposite-sex friendships similar to a dating relationship? (3) Have there ever been times when you felt that you would like an opposite-sex friendship to become a romantic relationship?

These questions were analyzed by using the method described in Section I. Specifically, responses to these questions were transcribed and thematized according to similarities in responses. Finally, excerpts from the interviews that best illustrated these themes were selected.

III. Survey Study of the Barriers to Close Cross-Sex Friendships (Werking, 1994a)

The participants in this study were 224 heterosexual men and women (122 women and 102 men) residing in a Midwestern city. The participants' ages ranged from 18 to 30 years (mean = 23.13 years). Fifty-one percent of the participants were in dating relationships, 23% were married, and 17% were not in a dating relationship at the time of the study. Forty-two percent of the participants attended college or had graduated from college, and 45% had not attended college but were high school graduates. None of the participants were engaged in a close cross-sex friendship at the time of the study, however, 82% reported having a close cross-sex friendship in the past. The average length of time since these friendships had ended was approximately 2 years.

The participants took part in one data collection session in which they responded in writing to a questionnaire (relevant sections of this survey are included in Appendix B). The survey consisted of a series of open- and closed-ended questions about why the participants did not have a close cross-sex friendship and why past cross-sex friendships had ended. The questionnaire also included Likert-type items assessing the respondents' perceptions of the nature of close cross-sex and same-sex friendships. Finally, respondents completed a series of demographic questions.

In order to determine the reasons for the absence of close cross-sex friendship, the participants' open-ended responses were categorized. These categories were developed by using Bulmer's (1979) method of analytic induction. This procedure involved developing categories based on a subsample of the data. These categories were then tested against the remaining data, and modifications in categories were made if needed. The resultant category scheme consisted of five major categories of reasons for the lack of cross-sex friendship. Two independent coders classified the responses by using this category scheme. Cohen's kappa estimate of intercoder reliability was .84.

IV. Survey Study of the Dissolution of Close Cross-Sex Friendships (Werking, 1994b)

Participants were 152 college students (83 women and 69 men) enrolled in communication and psychology courses at a Midwestern university, with an urban campus and a commuter student population. The participants' mean age was 24.3 years. The sample was composed primarily of white, middle-class, unmarried persons (71.7% were single). The described friendships lasted an average of 5 years.

The participants took part in one data collection session in which they responded in writing to a questionnaire (relevant questions from the survey are presented in Appendix B). The survey consisted of a series of open-ended questions and Likert-type items assessing the closeness of the friendships, the level of distress at the time of dissolution, and the participants' desire to renew the friendships. The questionnaire took approximately a half hour to complete.

The open-ended questions were categorized by using Bulmer's (1979) method of analytic induction. This procedure involved developing categories based on a subsample of the data. These categories were then tested against the remaining data, and modifications in the categories were made as needed. Two independent coders classified the responses to each open-ended question by using the categories developed for each question. Cohen's kappa estimate of intercoder reliability was .82 for the reasons for friendship termination, .83 for strategies for termination, .83 for dissemination of news to members of the friends' social networks, and .82 for the responses of members of the friends' social networks to this news.

V. Survey Study of the Talk and Activities of Close Cross-Sex Friends (Werking, 1994d)

Participants in this study were 170 men and women attending college at an urban university with a commuter population. The mean age of the respondents was 23 years. All of the participants were involved in a close cross-sex friendship at the time of the study. The average length of the reported friendships was 4.78 years.

The participants responded to a questionnaire that asked them to choose from a predetermined list the topics that they discuss with their cross-sex friends. This list was developed by research methods students at the same university and was piloted on a sample of 25 students to ascertain its completeness and validity. The respondents also listed the topics that they avoided talking about with their friends and provided the reasons that these topics were avoided. Finally, the respondents indicated from a predetermined list (this list was created in the same manner as the list of conversational topics) the friendship activities that they and their friends had done together during the month prior to the study. The questionnaire ended with a set of demographic questions. The survey took approximately 30 minutes to complete. The data were analyzed by calculating the frequency of occurrence of each conversational topic and activity.

Appendix B

Interview Protocols and Survey Questionnaires

I. Interviews with Pairs of Cross-Sex Friends

Individual Interview Protocol (Female Version*)

I. Instructions

First, I would like to explain the purpose of this interview and how it is organized. I am very interested in learning more about cross-sex friendships. In order to do this I would like to talk with you about cross-sex friendship in general and, in particular, your friendship with _____. There are no correct answers to these questions; I am interested in your thoughts and feelings about cross-sex friendship.

Your responses to the questions will be kept confidential, and I assure you that I will not divulge information from this interview to your cross-sex friend. In addition, your name will not be used in any reports I might develop as a result of this study. I will be tape-recording our interview so that I am not distracted by trying to write down information. Is that okay with you? Do you have any questions before we begin?

II. General Issues Regarding Cross-Sex Friendship

    1 a. What does the word "friendship" mean to you?
       b. When I say "cross-sex friendship," what does that mean to you?
    2. What expectations do you have of a male you would call a friend?

*The male version replaces "male" with "female" and male pronouns with female pronouns in the questions.

174

3. How many close friendships with males have you established other than your friendship with _____?

4 a. In general, how would you compare these friendships to your friendships with females?

b. How are these friendships similar to your friendships with females?

c. How are these friendships different from your friendships with females?

5. What have been some of the rewards of having cross-sex friends?

6 a. Have you ever been disappointed by your cross-sex friendships?

b. How have you handled those disappointments?

7. I'd like for you to think about the cross-sex friendships that you have had that did not last. Why did they end?

III. Specific Questions about Your Friendship with _____

Developmental Issues

8. How long have you and _____ been friends?

9. How did you and _____ meet?

10. Why do you think you and _____ "hit it off"?

11 a. How was your relationship initially defined? What sort of relationship was it?

b. How do you think _____ initially defined your relationship? Why?

12. What made you and _____ realize that you were friends? Was there a particular event or circumstance where you began to think of _____ as a friend?

13. Looking back on the friendship, can you identify different phases in your friendship? How has your friendship changed since it first began?

14. Have there been any important separations or breaks in the friendship?

General Information

15. What do you and _____ typically do when you are together?

16 a. What sorts of things do you and _____ talk about?

   b. Do you avoid talking about anything?

17 a. How does _____ communicate his affection for you?

   b. How do you communicate your affection for him?

18 a. How does _____ communicate his commitment to the friendship?

   b. How do you communicate your commitment to the friendship?

19 a. How does your friendship with _____ differ from a close friendship with a woman?

   b. How is it similar?

Legitimation of Relationship to Others

20 a. How does your friendship with _____ affect other relationships in which you are involved?

   b. How does your friendship with _____ affect other relationships in which _____ is involved?

21 a. How do other people respond to your friendship with _____?

   b. What do they ask you about your friendship?

   c. Why do you think they question you?

   d. What do you say to them in response to their reactions? How do you handle their reactions?

22. How have the reactions of other people affected your friendship? Please describe some specific examples.

Relationship Definition

23 a. Do you and _____ ever talk about your friendship?

   b. If so, were there particular events or issues that led you to talk about it?

24 a. Is there a relationship between cross-sex friendship and romance? (If so) What is the nature of that relationship?

   b. Have there ever been times when you felt you would like your friendship with _____ to become a romantic relationship?

   c. Have there been times when you have felt _____ was interested in becoming romantically involved with you?

d. How did you handle these situations?

e. Why do you think you have remained friends?

25 a. Have you ever felt as though _____ was sexually attracted to you?

b. How did you recognize his interest?

c. How did you react to his interest?

d. Have you ever felt sexually attracted to _____?

e. How did you feel about this attraction?

f. How did you and _____ handle these feelings?

Rituals/Relational Symbols of Cross-Sex Friendship

26 a. I'm interested in finding out about what makes your friendship with _____ unique. In particular, I'm interested in hearing about special objects, places, sayings, and so forth, which hold special meanings for you and _____.

b. As I was explaining what I'm interested in, did anything come to mind? Tell me about it. (Ask the following questions c–e for each symbol.)

c. How did this come to hold special significance in your friendship?

d. What does _____ mean to you?

e. What do you think it means to _____?

27 a. Can you describe activities that you and _____ do together at particular times each year?

b. How did this become a part of your friendship?

28 a. Are there things that you and _____ do together weekly?

b. How did this become a part of your weekly activities?

29 a. Are there things that you and _____ do together each time you are together?

b. How did this become a part of your time together?

Rewards/Difficulties in the Friendship

30 a. What do you like most about your friendship with _____?

b. What do you like least?

31 a. What do you think _____ likes most about your friendship?

b. What do you think _____ likes least?

32 a. Please describe particular times in your friendship when
   you have felt close with _____?

b. Times when you have felt distant?

33 a. Can you describe any problems you and _____have had
   that may have threatened your friendship?

b. How did you handle these problems?

34.   Is there anything you would change about your friendship
   with _____?

35.   Can you think of anything that would cause your friendship
   to end?

Cultural Images of Cross-Sex Friendship

36 a. Have you seen cross-sex friendship portrayed in movies,
   plays, television programs, magazine articles, or books?

b. *If so*, where?

c. Please describe the cross-sex friendship portrayed in
   _____. (Ask c–e for each portrayal they list.)

d. How is that portrayal of cross-sex friendship similar to
   your experience of friendship with _____?

e. How is it different?

f. In addition to the media, what other examples of cross-sex
   friendship have you seen?

g. *If not*, what examples of cross-sex friendship have you seen?

h. Do you know other persons who have a close cross-sex
   friendship?

i. Has anyone in your immediate family had close cross-sex
   friendships?

Metaphorical Description of Cross-Sex Friendship

37.   I would like you to describe your friendship with
   _____ using a metaphor. For example, if I asked you
   to describe your family metaphorically, you might say, "My
   family is a corporation" or "My family is like a baseball team."

Instructions: After selecting a metaphor for your friendship, I would then
like you to explain why you have chosen that particular metaphor. For
example, in explaining my use of a "corporation" to describe my family,

I might say, "My father is the CEO. My mother acts like the manager, carrying out my father's orders. And the kids are the workers, doing chores around the house."

38 a. Now I would like you to think of a metaphor that you think _____ would use in describing your friendship.

   b. Why do you think he would use this particular metaphor?

Conclusion

39.   Is there anything about your friendship with _____ that we have overlooked, but that you would like to mention?

Dyadic Interview Protocol

I. Instructions

From the information you gave me during the individual interviews, I have identified several issues in your friendship. Both of you spoke of these particular issues. (Go through list of issues.) I would like you to choose two issues you would like to talk about during this time together. Both of you must agree to discuss the issues. (Have them choose two.)

For each issue, ask the following questions:

1.   Why did you pick this particular issue?
2.   Please describe how this became an issue in your friendship.
3.   How does this issue affect your friendship?
4.   How have you tried to manage this issue?
5.   What would your relationship have been like if this issue did not exist?
6.   (If an ongoing issue) What would your friendship be like if the issue were resolved?

II. Instructions

I am going to leave the room and I would like for you to talk with one another while the tape-recorder is running. You can talk about anything you would like. I will return in about 10 minutes. Do you have any questions? (If they have questions about what to discuss, suggest when they first met or memorable events in the friendship.)

II. Survey Used for Identifying Barriers to Cross-Sex Friendships (Werking, 1994a)

1. Do you have a close opposite-sex friend currently?
   ____NO ____YES
2. If you answered NO to #1, please list the reason(s) why you do not have an opposite-sex friendship presently. Be as specific as possible.
3. Have you had a close opposite-sex friend in the past?
   ____NO ____YES
4. If you answered NO to #3, why do you think you have never had a close opposite-sex friend?

III. Survey Used for Investigating the Dissolution of Cross-Sex Friendships (Werking, 1994b)

1. Why do you think your friendship with this person ended?
2. How did you go about ending this friendship?
3. What were your feelings about the ending of this friendship at the time it ended?
4. What, if anything, could you have done to repair this friendship?
5. What did you tell other people (your friends, coworkers family) about the ending of your friendship?
6. What was the response of others when you told them about the ending of your friendship?

References

Abbey, A. (1982). Sex differences in attributions for friendly behavior: Do males misperceive females friendliness? *Journal of Personality and Social Psychology, 42,* 830–838.

Abbey, A. (1987). Misperceptions of friendly behavior as sexual interest: A survey of naturally occurring incidents. *Psychology of Women Quarterly, 11,* 173–194.

Adams, R. G. (1985). People would talk: Normative barriers to cross-sex friendships for elderly women. *The Gerontologist, 25,* 605–611.

Adams, R. G. (1989). Conceptual and methodological issues in studying friendships of older adults. In R. G. Adams & R. Blieszner (Eds.), *Older adult friendship* (pp. 17–41). Newbury Park, CA: Sage.

Allan, G. (1993). Social structure and relationships. In S. W. Duck (Ed.), *Social context and relationships* (pp. 1–25). Newbury Park, CA: Sage.

Altman, D. (1982). *The homosexualization of America.* Boston: Beacon.

Argyle, M., & Furnham, A. (1983). Sources of satisfaction and conflict in long-term relationships. *Journal of Marriage and the Family,* 481–493.

Argyle, M., & Henderson, M. (1985). The rules of relationships. In S. W. Duck & D. Perlman (Eds.), *Understanding personal relationships: An interdisciplinary approach* (pp. 63–85). London: Sage.

Aries, E. J., & Johnson, F. L. (1983). Close friendship in adulthood: Conversational content between same-sex friends. *Sex Roles, 9,* 1183–1196.

Arliss, L. (1993). When myths endure and realities change: Communication in romantic relationships. In L. Arliss & D. Borisoff (Eds.), *Women and men communicating* (pp. 71–85). New York: Harcourt Brace Jovanovich.

Aukett, R., Ritchie, J., & Mill, K. (1988). Gender differences in friendship patterns. *Sex Roles, 19,* 57–66.

Aune, K. S., & Comstock, J. (1991). Experience and expression of jealousy: Comparison between friends and romantics. *Psychological Reports, 69,* 315–319.

Babchuk, N. (1965). Primary friends and kin: A study of the associations of middle class couples. *Social Forces, 43,* 483–493.

Badhwar, N. K. (1987). Friends as ends in themselves. *Philosophy and Pheno-menological Research, XLVIII*(1), 1–23.

Bakan, D. (1966). *The duality of human existence.* Boston: Beacon.

Banikiotes, P. G., Neimeyer, G. J., & Lepkowsky, C. (1981). Gender and sex-role orientation effects on friendship choice. *Personality and Social Psychology Bulletin, 7,* 605–610.

Bateson, G. (1951). Information and codification: A philosophical approach. In J. Ruesch & G. Bateson (Eds.), *Communication: The social matrix of psychiatry* (pp. 168–211). New York: Norton.

Bateson, G. (1963). Exchange of information about patterns of human behavior. In W. S. Fields & W. Abbot (Eds.), *Information storage and neural control* (pp. 173–184). Springfield, IL: Charles C. Thomas.

Bateson, G. (1972a). Double bind, 1969. In *Steps to an ecology of mind* (pp. 448–465). New York: Ballantine.

Bateson, G. (1972b). The logical categories of learning and communica-tion. In *Steps to an ecology of mind* (pp. 279–308). New York: Ballan-tine.

Bateson, G. (1972c). A theory of play and fantasy. In *Steps to an ecology of mind* (pp. 177–193). New York: Ballantine.

Bateson, G. (1978). The pattern which connects. *Coevolutionary Quarterly, Summer,* 5–15.

Bateson, G. (1991a). The birth of a matrix, or double bind and epistemology. In R. E. Donaldson (Ed.), *A sacred unity: Further steps to an ecology of mind* (pp. 191–213). New York: HarperCollins.

Bateson, G. (1991b). A formal approach to explicit, implicit, and embodied ideas and to their forms of interaction. In R. E. Donaldson (Ed.), *A sacred unity: Further steps to an ecology of mind* (pp. 185–190). New York: HarperCollins.

Bateson, G. (1991c). The message of reinforcement. In R. E. Donaldson (Ed.), *A sacred unity: Further steps to an ecology of mind* (pp. 133–145). New York: HarperCollins.

Bateson, G. (1991d). Naven: Epilogue 1958. In R. E. Donaldson (Ed.), *A sacred unity: Further steps to an ecology of mind* (pp. 49–69). New York: HarperCollins.

Bateson, G. (1991e). Some components of socialization for trance. In R. E. Donaldson (Ed.), *A sacred unity: Further steps to an ecology of mind* (pp. 73–88). New York: HarperCollins.

Bateson, M. C. (1989). *Composing a life: Life as a work in progress. The improvisa-tions of five extraordinary women.* New York: Penguin.

Baxter, L. A. (1985). Accomplishing relationship disengagement. In S. W. Duck & D. Perlman (Eds.), *Understanding personal relationships: An interdiscipli-nary approach* (pp. 243–265). London: Sage.

Baxter, L. A. (1987). Symbols of relationship identity in relationship cultures. *Journal of Social and Personal Relationships, 4,* 261–280.

Baxter, L. A. (1992). Forms and functions of intimate play in personal relationships. *Human Communication Research, 18,* 336–363.

Baxter, L. A., & Wilmot, W. W. (1984). "Secret tests": Strategies for aquiring information about the state of the relationship. *Human Communication Research, 2,* 171–201.

Bell, R. R. (1981a). Friendships of women and of men. *Psychology of Women Quarterly, 5,* 402–417.

Bell, R. R. (1981b). *Worlds of friendship.* Beverly Hills, CA: Sage.

Bell, R. R., & Healey, J. G. (1992). Idiomatic communication and interpersonal solidarity in friends' relational cultures. *Human Communication Research, 18,* 307–335.

Bellah, R. N., Madsen, R., Sullivan, W. M., Swidler, A., & Tipton, S. M. (1985). *Habits of the heart: Individualism and commitment in American life.* San Francisco: Harper & Row.

Berger, P., & Kellner, H. (1964). Marriage and the construction of reality. *Diogenes, 46,* 1–24.

Bernard, J. (1976). Homosociality and female depression. *Journal of Social Issues, 32,* 213–238.

Berscheid, E., Snyder, M., & Omoto, A. (1989). Issues in studying close relationships: Conceptualizing and measuring closeness. In C. Hendrick (Ed.), *Close relationships* (pp. 63–91). Newbury Park, CA: Sage.

Block, J. D. (1980). *Friendship.* New York: Macmillan.

Bochner, A. P. (1981). Forming warm ideas. In C. Wilder-Mott & J. H. Weakland (Eds.), *Rigor and imagination: Essays from the legacy of Gregory Bateson* (pp. 65–81). New York: Praeger.

Bochner, A. P. (1982). On the efficacy of openness in close relationships. In M. Burgoon (Ed.), *Communication yearbook* (Vol. 5, pp. 109–124). New Brunswick, NJ: Transaction.

Bolton, C. D. (1959). *The development process in love relationships.* Unpublished doctoral dissertation, University of Chicago, Chicago, IL.

Bolton, C. D. (1961, August). Mate selection as the development of a relationship. *Marriage and Family Living,* pp. 234–240.

Booth, A., & Hess, E. (1974). Cross-sex friendship. *Journal of Marriage and the Family, 36,* 38–47.

Borisoff, D. J. (1993). The effect of gender on establishing and maintaining intimate relationships. In L. T. Arliss & D. J. Borioff (Eds.), *Women and men communicating: Challenges and changes* (pp. 14–28). New York: Harcourt Brace Jovanovich.

Brain, R. (1976). *Friends and lovers.* New York: Basic Books.

Bringle, R. G., & Boebinger, K. L. G. (1990). Jealousy and the "third" person in the love triangle. *Journal of Social and Personal Relationships, 7,* 119–133.

Bringle, R. G., & Buunk, B (1985). Jealousy and social behavior: A review of person, relationship and situational determinants. In P. Shaver (Ed.), *Review of personality and social psychology: Vol. 6. Self, situations, and social behavior.* Beverly Hills, CA: Sage.

Buhrke, R. A., & Fuqua, D. R. (1987). Sex differences in same- and cross-sex supportive relationships. *Sex Roles, 17,* 339–351.

Bukowski, W. M., Nappi, B. J., & Hoza, B. (1988). A test of Aristotle's model of friendship for young adults' same-sex and opposite-sex relationships. *Journal of Social Psychology, 127,* 595–603.

Bulmer, M. (1979). Concepts in the analysis of qualitative data. *Sociological Review, 27,* 651–677.

Burleson, B. R., Kunkel, A. W., Samter, W., & Werking, K. J. (1996). Men's and women's evaluations of communication skills in personal relationships: When sex differences make a difference—and when they don't. *Journal of Social and Personal Relationships, 13,* 201–224.

Caldwell, M. A., & Peplau, L. A. (1982). Sex differences in same-sex friendship. *Sex Roles, 8,* 721–732.

Candy, S. G., Troll, L. E., & Levy, S. G. (1981). A developmental exploration of friendship functions in women. *Psychology of Women Quarterly, 5,* 456–472.

Cates, R. M., & Lloyd, S. A. (1992). *Courtship.* Newbury Park, CA: Sage.

Chown, S. M. (1981). Friendship in old age. In S. Duck & R. Gilmour (Eds.), *Personal relationships: Vol. 2. Developing personal relationships* (pp. 231–246). New York: Academic.

Chafetz, J. S. (1974). *Masculine/feminine or human?* Itasca, IL: Peacock.

Cohen, J. J., D'Heurle, A., & Widmark-Petersson, V. (1980). Cross-sex friendship in children: Gender patterns and cultural perspectives. *Psychology in the Schools, 17,* 523–529.

Crawford, M. (1977). What is a friend? *New Sociology, 20,* 116–117.

Davidson, L. R., & Duberman, L. (1982). Friendship: Communication and interactional patterns in same-sex dyads. *Sex Roles, 8,* 809–822.

Davis, K. E., & Todd, M. J. (1982). Friendship and love relationships. In K. Davis (Ed.), *Advances in descriptive psychology* (Vol. 2, pp. 79–122). Greenwich, CT: JAI.

Davis, K. E., & Todd, M. J. (1985). Assessing friendship: Prototypes, paradigm cases and relationship description. In S. W. Duck & D. Perlman. (Eds.), *Understanding personal relationships: An interdisciplinary approach* (pp. 17–38). London: Sage.

Deaux, K., & Major, B. (1987). Putting gender into context: An interactive model of gender-related behavior. *Psychological Review, 94,* 369–389.

de Beauvoir, S. (1952). *The second sex*. New York: Vintage.

Delia, J. G. (1980). Some tentative thoughts concerning the study of interpersonal relationships and their development. *Western Journal of Speech Communication, 44,* 97–103.

Denzin, N. K. (1978). The logic of naturalistic inquiry. In N. K. Denzin (Ed.), *Sociological methods: A sourcebook* (pp. 6–29). New York: McGraw-Hill.

Denzin, N. K. (1989). *Interpretive interactionism.* Newbury Park, CA: Sage.

DiIorio, J. A. (1989). Being and becoming coupled: The emergence of female subordination in heterosexual relationships. In B. Risman & P. Schwartz, (Eds.), *Gender in intimate relationships* (pp. 94–107). Belmont, CA: Wadsworth.

Duck, S. (1982). A topography of relationship disengagement and dissolution. In S. W. Duck (Ed.) *Personal relationships: Vol. 4. Dissolving personal relationships* (pp. 1–30). London: Academic.

Duck, S. (1990). Relationships as unfinished business: Out of the frying pan and into the 1990s. *Journal of Social and Personal Relationships, 7,* 5–28.

Duck, S. (1994). *Meaningful relationships: Talking, sense, and relating.* Thousand Oaks, CA: Sage.

Duck, S. W., & Wright, P. H. (1993). Reexamining gender differences in same-gender friendships: A close look at two kinds of data. *Sex Roles, 28,* 709–727.

Dweck, C. S. (1981). Social-cognitive processes in children's friendships. In S. R. Asher & J. M. Gottman (Eds.), *The development of children's friendships.* Cambridge, MA: Cambridge University Press.

Ellin, A. (1993). Just friends: Can men and women do it without doing it? *Utne Reader, 55,* pp. 66–67.

Faderman, L. (1989). A history of romantic friendship and lesbian love. In B. J. Risman & P. Schwartz (Eds.), *Gender in intimate relationships: A microstructural approach* (pp. 26–310). Belmont, CA. Wadsworth.

Fasteau, N. D. (1975). *The male machine.* New York: Delta.

Francoeur, R., & Francoeur, A. (1977). Hot and cool sex: Fidelity in marriage. In R. Libby & R. Whitehurst (Eds.), *Marriage and alternatives: Exploring intimate relationships* (pp. 302–318). Glenview, IL: Scott, Foresman.

Furman, L. G. (1986). *Cross-gender friendships in the workplace: Factors and components.* Unpublished doctoral dissertation, Fielding Institute, ND.

Gadlin, H. (1977). Private lives and public order: A critical view of the history of intimate relations in the United States. In G. Levinger & H. Rausch (Eds.), *Close relationships: Perspectives on the meaning of intimacy* (pp. 33–71). Amherst: University of Massachusetts Press.

Geertz, C. (1976). From the native's point of view: On the nature of anthropological understanding. In K. H. Basso & H. A. Selby (Eds.), *Meaning in anthropology* (pp. 221–237). Albuquerque: University of New Mexico Press.

Gergen, K. J. (1980). Toward generative theory. *Journal of Personality and Social Psychology, 36,* 1344–1360.

Gilligan, C. (1982). *In a different voice: Psychological theory and women's development.* Cambridge MA: Harvard University Press.

Gottman, J. M. (1982). Temporal form: Toward a new language for describing relationships. *Journal of Marriage and Family, 44,* 943–962.

Gottman, J. M. (1986). The world of coordinated play: Same- and cross-sex friendship in young children. In J. M. Gottman & J. G. Parker (Eds.), *Conversations of friends: Speculations on affective development* (pp. 139–191). Cambridge, MA: Cambridge University Press.

Gottman, J. M., & Mettetal, G. (1986). Speculations about social and affective development: Friendship and acquaintanceship through adolescence. In J. M. Gottman & J. G. Parker (Eds.), *Conversations of friends: Speculations on affective development* (pp. 192–237). Cambridge, MA: Cambridge University Press.

Grauerholz, E., & Serpe, R. T. (1985). Initiation and response: The dynamics of sexual interactions. *Sex Roles, 12,* 1041–1059.

Hacker, H. M. (1981). Blabbermouths and clams: Sex differences in self-disclosure in same-sex and cross-sex friendship dyads. *Psychology of Women Quarterly, 5,* 385–401.

Haley, J. (1963). *Strategies of psychotherapy.* New York: Grune & Stratton.

Hendrick, S., & Hendrick, C. (1992). *Romantic love.* Newbury Park, CA: Sage.

Hess, B. (1972). Friendship. In M. W. Riley, M. Johnson, & A. Foner (Eds.), *Aging and society* (pp. 357–393). New York: Russell Sage Foundation.

Hochschild, A. R. (1979). Emotion work, feeling rules, and social structure. *American Journal of Sociology, 85,* 551–575.

Hopper, R., Knapp, M. L., & Scott, L. (1981). Couples' personal idioms: Exploring intimate talk. *Journal of Communication, 31,* 23–33.

Horton, M. (1973). Alternatives to romantic love. In M. E. Curtin (Ed.), *Symposium on love* (pp. 107–121). New York: Behavioral Publications.

Johnson, F. L., & Aries, E. J. (1983). The talk of women friends. *Women's Studies International Forum, 6,* 353–361.

Kamarovsky, M. (1974). Patterns of self-disclosure of male undergraduates. *Journal of Marriage and the Family, 36,* 677–686.

Kon, I., & Losenkov, V. A. (1978). Friendship in adolescence: Values and behavior. *Journal of Marriage and the Family, 40,* 143–55.

Lampe, P. E. (1985). Friendship and adultery. *Sociological Inquiry, 55*(3), 310–324.

Lannamann, J. W. (1991). Interpersonal communication research as ideological practice. *Communication Theory, 1,* 179–203.

Larson, L. (1974). System and subsystem perception of family roles. *Journal of Marriage and the Family, 36,* 123–138.

Laws, J. L., & Schwartz, P. (1981). *Sexual scripts: The social construction of female sexuality.* Washington, DC: University Press of America.

Lopata, H. Z. (1981). Friendship: Historical and theoretical introduction. In H. Z. Lopata (Ed.), *Research in the interweave of social roles: Vol. 2. Friendship.* Greenwich, CT: JAI.

Maccoby, E. (1988). Gender as a social category. *Developmental Psychology, 24,* 755–765.

Mahoney, J., & Heretick, D. M. L. (1979). Factor-specific dimensions in person perception for same- and opposite-sex friendship dyads. *The Journal of Social Psychology, 107,* 219–225.

Maines, D. R. (1982). In search of mesostructure: Studies in the negotiated order. *Urban Life, 11,* 267–279.

Maines, D. R. (1989). Further dialectics: Strangers, friends and historical transformations. *Communication yearbook* (Vol. 12, pp. 190–202). Newbury, CA: Sage.

Malone, J. W. (1980). *Straight women/gay men.* New York: Dial.

McCall, G. (1988). The organizational life cycle of relationships. In S. W. Duck (Ed.), *Handbook of personal relationships* (pp. 467–484). New York: Wiley.

McKinney, K. (1987). Age and gender differences in college students' attitudes toward women: A replication and extension. *Sex Roles, 17,* 353–358.

Milardo, R. M., Johnson, M. P., & Huston, T. L. (1983). Developing close relationships: Changing patterns of interaction between pair members and social networks. *Journal of Personality and Social Psychology, 44,* 964–976.

Monsour, M. (1992). Meanings of intimacy in cross- and same-sex friendships. *Journal of Social and Personal Relationships, 9,* 277–295.

Montgomery, B. M. (1981). The form and function of quality communication in marriage. *Family Relations, 30,* 21–30.

Nardi, P. M. (1992). Sex, friendship, and gender roles among gay men. In P. Nardi (Ed.), *Men's friendships* (pp. 173–185). Newbury Park, CA: Sage.

Nardi, P. M., & Sherrod, D. (1994). Friendship in the lives of gay men and lesbians. *Journal of Social and Personal Relationships, 11,* 185–199.

Nestle, J., & Preston, J. (1994). *Sister and brother: Lesbians and gay men write about their lives together.* San Francisco: HarperCollins.

O'Connor, P. (1992). *Friendships between women: A critical review.* New York: Guilford.

Oliker, S. J. (1989). *Best friends and marriage: Exchange among women.* Berkeley: University of California Press.

O'Meara, J. D. (1989). Cross-sex friendship: Four basic challenges of an ignored relationship. *Sex Roles, 21,* 525–543.

O'Meara, J. D. (1994). Cross-sex friendship's opportunity challenge: Uncharted terrain for exploration. *Personal Relationship Issues, 2,* 4–7.

Orbuch, T. L. (1992). A symbolic interactionist approach to the study of relationship loss. In T. L. Orbuch (Ed.), *Close relationship loss: Theoretical approaches.* New York: Springer-Verlag.

Paine, R. (1974). An exploratory analysis in "middle-class" culture. In E. Leylon (Ed.), *The compact: Selected dimensions of friendship* (pp. 117–137). St. John's: Institute of Social and Economic Research.

Parker, S., & de Vries, B. (1993). Patterns of friendship for women and men in same- and cross-sex relationships. *Journal of Social and Personal Relationships, 10,* 617–626.

Parks, M. R. (1982). Ideology in interpersonal communication: Off the couch and into the world. In M. Burgoon (Ed.), *Communication yearbook* (Vol. 5, pp. 79–107). New Brunswick, NJ: Transaction.

Parlee, M. B. (1979). The friendship bond. *Psychology Today, 13,* 43–54.

Pogrebin, L. (1987). *Among friends.* New York: McGraw-Hill.

Rands, M., & Levinger, G. (1979). Implicit theories of relationship: An intergenerational study. *Journal of Personality and Social Psychology, 37,* 645–661.

Rawlins, W. K. (1981). *Friendship as a communicative achievement: A theory and an interpretive analysis of verbal reports.* Unpublished doctoral dissertation, Temple University, Philadelphia, PA.

Rawlins, W. K. (1982). Cross-sex friendship and the communicative management of sex-role expectations. *Communication Quarterly, 30,* 343–352.

Rawlins, W. K. (1983a). Negotiating close friendship: The dialectic of conjunctive freedoms. *Human Communication Research, 9,* 255–266.

Rawlins, W. K. (1983b). Openness as problematic in ongoing friendships: Two conversational dilemmas. *Communication Monographs, 50,* 1–13.

Rawlins, W. K. (1987). Gregory Bateson and the composition of human communication. *Research on Language and Social Interaction, 20,* 53–77.

Rawlins, W. K. (1989a). Cultural double agency and the pursuit of friendship. *Cultural Dynamics, 11,* 28–40.

Rawlins, W. K. (1989b). A dialectical analysis of the tensions, functions, and strategic challenges of communication in young adult friendships. In J. A. Anderson (Ed.), *Communication yearbook* (Vol. 12, pp. 157–189). Newbury, CA: Sage.

Rawlins, W. K. (1992). *Friendship matters: Communication, dialectics, and the life course.* New York: Aldine De Gruyter.

Rawlins, W. K. (1993). Communication in cross-sex friendships. In L. P. Arliss & D. J. Borisoff (Eds.), *Women and men communicating* (pp. 51–70). Orlando, FL: Holt, Rinehart & Winston.

Rawlins, W. K. (1994). Reflecting on cross-sex friendship: De-scripting the drama. *Personal Relationships Issues, 2,* 1–3.

Rawlins, W. K., & Holl, M. (1988). Adolescents' interactions with parents and friends: Dialectics of temporal perspective and evaluation. *Journal of Social and Personal Relationships, 5,* 27–46.

Raymond, J. G. (1986). *A passion for friends: Toward a philosophy of female affection.* Boston: Beacon.

Reisman, J. M. (1981). Adult friendships. In S. Duck & R. Gilmour (Eds.), *Personal relationships: Vol. 2. Developing personal relationships* (pp. 205–230). London: Sage.

Roberts, M. K. (1982). Men and women: Partners, lovers, friends. In K. E. Davis & T. Mitchell (Eds.), *Advances in descriptive psychology* (Vol. 2, pp. 57–78). Greenwich, CT: JAI.

Rorty, R. (1979). *Philosophy and the mirror of nature.* Princeton: Princeton University Press.

Rose, S. M. (1984). How friendships end: Patterns among young adults. *Journal of Social and Personal Relationships, 1,* 267–277.

Rose, S. M. (1985). Same- and cross-sex friendships and the psychology of homosociality. *Sex Roles, 12,* 63–74.

Rose, S. M., & Serafica, F. C. (1986). Keeping and ending casual, close and best friendships. *Journal of Social and Personal Relationships, 3,* 275–288.

Rubin, L. B. (1985). *Just friends.* New York: Harper & Row.

Sapadin, L. A. (1988). Friendship and gender: Perspectives of professional men and women. *Journal of Social and Personal Relationships, 5,* 387–403.

Sharabany, R., Gershoni, R., & Hofman, J. E. (1981). Girlfriend, boyfriend: Age and sex differences in intimate friendship. *Developmental Psychology, 17,* 800–808.

Simmel, G. (1971). *On individuality and social forms* (edited and with an introduction by D. N. Levine). Chicago: University of Chicago Press.

Simpson, J. A., Campbell, B., & Berscheid, E. (1986). The association between romantic love and marriage: Kephart (1967) twice revisited. *Personality and Social Psychology Bulletin, 12,* 363–372.

Smith, A. B., & Inder, P. M. (1990). The relationship of classroom organization to cross-age and cross-sex friendships. *Educational Psychology, 10,* 127–140.

Suttles, G. D. (1970). Friendship as a social institution. In G. J. McCall, M. M. McCall, N. K. Denzin, G. D. Suttles, & S. B. Kurth (Eds.), *Social relationships* (pp. 95–135). Chicago: Aldine.

Swain, S. O. (1992). Men's friendships with women: Intimacy, sexual boundaries, and the informant role. In P. Nardi (Ed.), *Men's friendships* (pp. 153–171). Newbury Park, CA: Sage.

Tannen, D. (1990). *You just don't understand: Women and men in conversation.* New York: Morrow.

Taylor, C. (1977). Interpretation and the sciences of man. In F. R. Dallmayr & T. A. McCarthy (Eds.), *Understanding and social inquiry* (pp. 101–131). South Bend, IN: University of Notre Dame Press.

Tesch, S. A., & Martin, R. R. (1983). Friendship conceptions of young adults in two age groups. *Journal of Psychology, 115,* 7–12.

Thompson, L., & Walker, A. J. (1982). The dyad as the unit of analysis: Conceptual and methodological issues. *Journal of Marriage and the Family, 44,* 889–900.

Thorne, B. (1986). Girls and boys together . . . but mostly apart: Gender arrangements in elementary schools. In W. Hartup & Z. Rubin (Eds.), *Relationships and development* (pp. 167–184). Hillsdale, NJ: Erlbaum.

Ting-Toomey, S. (1989). Culture and interpersonal relationship development: Some conceptual issues. In J. A. Anderson (Ed.), *Communication yearbook* (Vol. 12, pp. 371–382). Newbury, CA: Sage.

Van de Vate, D. (1981). *Romantic love: A philosophical inquiry.* University Park: Pennsylvania State University Press.

Vaughan, D. (1986). *Uncoupling: Turning points in intimate relationships.* New York: Oxford University Press.

Weinstein, R. K. (1982). The process of termination in intimate same-sex friendships. *Dissertation Abstracts International, 43,* 2154-B.

Weiss, L., & Lowenthal, M. F. (1975). Life-course perspective on friendship. In M. Thurnber & D. Chiriboga (Eds.), *Four stages of life.* San Francisco: Jossey-Bass.

Werking, K. J. (1990, November). *Communicative challenges of cross-sex friendship: Managing the public image of an anomic relationship.* Paper presented at the Speech Communication Association Convention, Chicago, IL.

Werking, K. J. (1992). *The communicative management of cross-sex friendship.* Unpublished dissertation, Purdue University.

Werking, K. J. (1994a, May). *Barriers to the formation of cross-sex friendship.* Paper presented at the INPR Professional Development Conference, Iowa City, IA.

Werking, K. J. (1994b, November). *Dissolving cross-sex friendships.* Paper presented at the Speech Communication Association Convention, New Orleans, LA.

Werking, K. J. (1994c). *Distinguishing cross-sex friendship from heterosexual romantic relationships.* Unpublished manuscript, University of Louisville, Louisville, KY.

Werking, K. J. (1994d). *The talk and activities of close cross-sex friends.* Unpublished manuscript, University of Louisville, Louisville, KY.

Werking, K. J. (1995, October). *Media portrayals of cross-sex friendship.* Paper presented at the Organization for the Study of Culture, Language and Gender, Minneapolis, MN.

Werking, K. J. (1996). Cross-sex friendship research as ideological practice. In S. W. Duck (Ed.), *Handbook of personal relationships* (2nd ed.). West Sussex, UK: Wiley.

West, C., & Fenstermaker, S. (1995). Doing difference. *Gender and Society, 9,* 8–37.

Weston, K. (1991). *Families we choose.* New York: Columbia University Press.

Whitney, C. (1990). *Uncommon lives: Gay men and straight women.* New York: New American Library.

Wilmot, W. W. (1980). Metacommunication: A re-examination and extension. In D. Nimmo (Ed.), *Communication yearbook* (Vol. 4, pp. 61–69). New Brunswick, NJ: Transaction.

Wilson, T. P. (1970). Conceptions of interaction and forms of sociological explanation. *American Sociological Review, 35,* 697–709.

Wiseman, J. P. (1986). Friendship: Bonds and binds in a voluntary relationship. *Journal of Social and Personal Relationships, 3,* 191–211.

Wood, J. T. (1993). Engendered relations: Interaction, caring, power, and responsibility in intimacy. In S. Duck (Ed.), *Social context and relationships* (pp. 26–54). Newbury Park, CA: Sage.

Wright, P. H. (1982). Men's friendships, women's friendships and the alleged inferiority of the latter. *Sex Roles, 8,* 1–20.

Wright, P. H. (1988). Interpreting research on gender differences in friendship: A case for moderation and a plea for caution. *Journal of Social and Personal Relationships, 5,* 367–373.

Wright, P. H. (1989). Gender differences in adults' same- and cross–gender friendships. In R. G. Adams & R. Blieszner (Eds.), *Older adult friendship* (pp. 197–221). Newbury Park, CA: Sage.

Wright, P. H., & Bergloff, P. J. (1984, June). *The acquaintance description form and the comparative study of personal relationships.* Paper presented at the Second International Conference on Personal Relationships, Madison, WI.

Youniss, J., & Smollar, J. (1985). *Adolescent relations with mothers, fathers, and friends.* Chicago: University of Chicago Press.

Index